WEIGHED
AND
FOUND
WANTING

*An Analysis of Major Evangelical Political
Engagement in America (Vol.1)*

Ricky V. Kyles Sr., DEdMin.

ISBN 978-1-64468-789-5 (Paperback)
ISBN 978-1-63885-590-3 (Hardcover)
ISBN 978-1-64468-790-1 (Digital)

Covenant Books, Inc.
11661 Hwy 707
Murrells Inlet, SC 29576
www.covenantbooks.com

DEDICATION

Even as I acknowledge the many people who have been instrumental in my formation, there are always people, and then there are *people*. James and Ethel Kyles, my beloved parents, constitute *the people* in my life. Yes, it is only through Jesus Christ that I *live, move, and have my being*. That is the vertical perspective, and nothing comes close or compares but, God ordains both the ends as well as the means. His means for me were a simple country boy and gal from a little nondescript place, Brooksville, Mississippi.

It is ironic because they did so in profoundly different ways and at different times. My mom was the catalyst during my early years, and when she passed, my dad and I went through an awkward phase, probably based on the adjustment both of us had to endure. Yet thankfully, that period only lasted a short time as when I started to raise my own family, my relationship with my father morphed into an almost idyllic father and son bond. Both my mom and dad taught me so much, and I am the blessed recipient of a mom and dad who poured every ounce of love, counsel, and support that was endowed from God above.

Both my parents were raised in Mississippi during the *Jim Crow* times, so they were not afforded many of the privileges and opportunities I was blessed to enjoy. I can still remember receiving a letter from my father while I was attending basic training. My dad's letter was filled with spelling and punctuation errors, but my father took the time to express how proud he was of me. Even though my mom died shortly after my college graduation, I can still see the look of admiration and pride on her face at my graduation. Her smile remains indelibly etched in my mind. Our relationship was unique: my mother was my best friend while growing up, hoping to become a man, and my father became my best friend as I labored to become that man.

I know it is anticlimactic for anyone to posit their parents were the greatest and a little unrealistic as there is no real way to quantify or falsify such a bodacious claim. So I will only postulate this: James Earl and Ethel Lynn Bardley Kyles were the most exquisitely qualified parents that God knew it would take to conform me to the image of His Dear Son, Jesus Christ of Nazareth! In short, Ricky Verndale Kyles received the perfect parents, uniquely suited just for him. Who wouldn't learn to thank and serve a God like this?

The Westminster Shorter Catechism posits the following Q and A:

Q: What is the chief end of man?
A: Man's chief end is to glorify God, and to enjoy him forever.

I hope this book, along with other events and actions, allow me to accomplish this stated chief end. Immediately after experiencing this chief end, I hope to enjoy a great reunion with these two people who have been so instrumental in my formation. Whereas on this side of the River Jordan, the time was but a vapor, the time on the other side of the Jordan will be endless *howdys, howdys*, and never good-bye.

CONTENTS

ACKNOWLEDGMENTS

A wise steward understands they are never an island unto themselves. They understand they are truly indebted to a multitude of peoples that have contributed to the person they are currently and still aspire to be. Thus, I am no different; my life has been blessed beyond repayment by so many throughout the years.

It is always dicey to single out people as you are sure to disappoint whoever name you leave out, but being fully aware of the risk I proceed, nonetheless. Everything in my life starts with James Earl and Ethel Lynn Kyles, my father, and my mother. My mother was the central most influential person in my young formative years, and my father became my rock as I grew older, especially after my mother passed, and I began to raise my own family. My biggest regret is that they will not be alive to share in this accomplishment, to whatever degree this enterprise is successful, but eternity awaits for us to bask in that delayed delight.

I have blessed to have many strong females shower me with unconditional love aside from my mother to include both my maternal and paternal grandmothers, Julia Bardley, and Susie Kyles. To whatever degree the final chapter of my earthly pilgrimage has something positive to say about me, a lot of that credit will be due to their doting love for me. Countless aunts, starting with my Aunt Minnie, have always made me feel as if I was their favorites and were among my constant cheerleaders, even during times when I did not deserve any cheers.

I have equally blessed by many positive male experiences aside from my father. The entire list would be too long to enumerate, but I just want to express my eternal thanks to Pastors Wesley Conner and Daniel Gute, along with Deacons Isaiah Brinker and Samuel

Thompson. I would be remiss if I did not mention some of the males who are closer in age and have been with me every step of the way. They are my college roommates, Brigadier General Rodney C. Boyd Sr. and Paul B. Cox Sr, along with Robert Hatcher. We met as pledges way back in the fall semester of 1983, and my life has never been the same. I share a deep bond with my biological brother and subsequent fraternity brother, Rodney Kyles, and his friendship has been unwavering even when we do not always agree.

I thank my wife, Monique, and my children, who have been with me every step of the journey and, I would like to especially thank my son, Ricky Jr., for his continual encouragement as I pursued this endeavor. Ricky Jr., you will never fully understand how your joy and pride gave me the extra juice to keep pressing on.

I reserve my final words for Brother Dr. James G. A. Mendez Jr. I first contemplated the idea to work this book about a year and a half ago. Still, I would often become dismayed as not being able to tackle such a formidable task. Yet, James' continual prodding and inquiries regarding my progress provided me with the resolve to see the job through to completion. The fact that James was able to author his own book gave me the confidence that I was worthy to meet the task because that is what the men of *Alpha Phi Alpha Fraternity Inc.* do. Sometimes it comes down to someone else believing in you more than you believe in yourself at the time. Eventually, I had to embrace the challenge head-on, but frankly, I do not likely get there without James's support. So although James and I differ on so many issues, I still regard and value him as a dear, dear friend.

All of these acknowledgments are authentic, heartfelt, and well-deserved, but they are always derivative. Meaning they do not derive from any inherent attribute of the person. They only take place because of the grace and mercy Jesus Christ of Nazareth has bestowed upon a wretched sinner like me. To the degree this book grants glory and honor to God, I write as one with fear and trembling, realizing that each and every one of us will one day stand before God and give an account.

I hope this book is part of the material God is able to find me *weighed and not wanting*. It will be only then that it can be said my living on this side of the River Jordan was not in vain.

In His Grip,
Dr. Ricky Verndale Kyles Sr.

INTRODUCTION

Casting down imaginations, and every high thing that
exalteth itself against the knowledge of God, and bringing
into captivity every thought to the obedience of Christ.
—2 Cor. 10:5 (KJV)

A religion that cannot take a lick ain't worth a lick.
—Susie Kyles

So many traits and principles have served me well due to of twenty-eight years of military service for which I will always be grateful. Noble and necessary traits like accountability, loyalty, and respect have been instrumental in my formation and have allowed me to achieve a modicum of success. One of the principles that have been especially insightful for me is the principle known by the acronym: BLUF. BLUF stands for "Bottom Line Up Front." The BLUF principle means you do not waste time but cut right to the chase due to the reality the person on the receiving end of the information (in a military context, usually a general or some other high-ranking individual) did not have nor would not grant you a lot of time. Hence, you needed to make your point succinct and quickly. Similarly, it is imperative if an author of a book or director of a film is to capture the audience's attention, they must do it in the first three-five minutes or, they dramatically increase the likelihood of losing their audience.

In that vein, let me attempt to grab your attention so you might be more inclined to be absorbed in dialogue with me. My thesis statement, my BLUF, is that no African American Evangelical in the United States of America should politically align themselves with the Democratic Party as they are presently constituted. To avoid any confusion, let me state in the most explicit terms possible, I do not believe an African American Evangelical in the USA can posit biblical fidelity and vote in any election of any consequence (which is virtually *any* election at *any* level, be it the local, state or national level) for a political candidate from the Democratic Party as it stands today.

I stand as one flabbergasted that 94 percent of African American Evangelicals voted for President Barack Obama and 88 percent of African American Evangelicals voted for Democratic Presidential Candidate Hilary Rodman Clinton.[1] I believe the Democratic Party has essentially become a godless institution. Their level of godlessness continues to increase at a disturbing frequency that seems to take place without any indication of positive change on the horizon. Recent action like the Democratic Party's rejection of the *Born-Alive Abortion Survivor Protection Act* is a vivid indicator of the degree to which the Democratic Party has fully embraced an anti-God moral revolution.

One may wonder why a seemingly insignificant individual with no special qualifications or pedigree would dare enter his voice into a controversial and taboo subject as politics coupled with religion. Many in the culture, especially high culture, postulate these are the two forbidden topics proper people are told from as we begin to enter adulthood to never bring up in polite conversation. It is repeated and modeled so frequently you would swear it finds its source from the mouth of God Himself, if one even dares to believe such a Person exists, or at the very least from the lips of some venerated sage. It is so ingrained within our culture to such a degree that Evangelicals seem to enthusiastically accept it as *part and parcel* of their Evangelical worldview. Now, I would be one of the first to agree that much care and charity needs to accompany such a potentially explosive public discourse. Far too often more heat than light easily dominates

---

[1] This statement is not an unfiltered endorsement of the Republican Party. I did not vote for Presidential Candidate Donald Trump in 2020 as I believe a consistent Evangelical would find a similar disqualification of Presidential Candidate Donald Trump. What is good for the goose must be good for the gander in this case. It is my hope to write a companion volume to this work, but I feel a responsibility to speak to my own house before I speak to another context.

the conversation. Regrettably, we have lost the art of pointed but civil discourse. Yet I believe Evangelicals have unnecessarily ceded the high ground when Evangelicals consciously shy away from those potentially uncomfortable conversations, with friends and foes alike.

Many Evangelicals will readily recognize the biblical citation that begins this chapter. It is frequently quoted and is one of my favorite passages in the entire Holy Writ. It is part of how I am *wired* as an individual. I am an *alpha male* who likes to mix it up. I immensely love a spirited back and forth discussion, be the topic sports or politics and even some of the finer theological doctrinal points that cause so much consternation within the Body of Christ. One of my many frustrations of our culture in general and of the Evangelical culture, in particular, is the biblical motif of Manhood has been emasculated to such an alarming rate that even the Church does not unapologetically present Christ in all of His Personhood, his entire Manhood, so to speak.

It seems perfectly acceptable to present Christ as the Suffering Servant, as the Paschal Lamb, as the Babe in the Manger and He is certainly at least all of those things, yet it is equally true He is the roaring Lion from the Tribe of Judah. He is the Rose of Sharon; He is the conquering King who is soon to return to vanquish all of His foes. Many love to quote, *"A bruised reed He will not crush"* (Matt. 12:20) but how many also realize He is also the same individual who said, *"But as for these enemies of mine, who did not want me to reign over them, bring them here and **slaughter them** before me"* (Luke 19:27, emphasis mine). It is understandable when people who are not committed to the actual teachings of the Bible do not fully understand, embrace and proclaim an accurate picture of our great Savior but, I believe there is a lack of precision in the average Evangelical's understanding concerning the full Personhood of Christ. Engage in a dialogue with the average Evangelical and they will speak effusively about the love of Christ, but you will nary hear much about the wrath of Christ. You simply do not have one without the other. In fact, I believe when Evangelicals seek to evangelize the lost, we should lead with the wrath of God without apology. Frankly, I believe the Gospel is most powerfully communicated when we provide a sufficient context where divine deliverance is desperately needed. The Church fails to create the proper sense of desperation when we make Jesus Christ akin to a *best buddy* to help us navigate the temporal affairs of this world.

Instead of a warm and fuzzy sanitized appeal, one finds the Gospel message to be, *"This Jesus delivered up according to the definite plan and foreknowledge of God, you crucified and killed... Now when they heard this, they were pierced to the heart, and said to Peter and the rest of the apostles, "Brethren, what shall we do?"* The Apostle Peter then delivered a truncated but fully efficient Gospel invitation when he said, *"Repent, and let each of you be baptized in the name of Jesus Christ for the forgiveness of your sins; and you shall receive the gift of the Holy Spirit"* (Acts 2:23ff). The Evangelical Church has tragically domesticated the Gospel that results in the bastardization of God's Holiness and the Sinfulness of Man. The Gospel is no longer an offense. It is wholly therapeutic in nature. Fallen man does not need therapy; we desperately need Divine Rescue. Yet, the radical embrace of a need for Divine Rescue is alien (even hostile to many) to those who naively believe nothing is awaiting them but *Ease in Zion.*

When we speak intramurally among fellow believers, we must not minimize or even in many cases neglect to speak much about the *holiness of God* and the *sinfulness of man.* I believe Evangelicals, in many cases but certainly not all, lack the moral courage to have that honest conversation, even among fellow believers, they attend Church with and worship God. Sometimes, due to a lack of confidence, they possess the intellectual acumen from an exegetical perspective to hold their own when they dialogue with others.[2] Other times it is because they do not believe it that important of an issue, so they adopt a posture of apathy because it does not directly impact (or so they tragically believe) their day-to-day lives. Finally, some refrain from entering the fray because they do not want to risk the loss of

---

[2]   Exegesis is the biblical interpretation principle whereby we derive from the text what it says and thus what it means. As opposed to eisegesis where the meaning is read into the text. In exegesis we are only concerned about what the author meant by what he communicated to the original audience. In eisegesis the reader controls the meaning.

influence and favor with the people in their sphere of influence. They do so in direct antithesis to the example of Christ when God inspired the historian and Gospel writer Luke to write, *"And Jesus increased in wisdom and in stature and in favor with God and man"* (Luke 2:52). Jesus Christ never shied away from speaking the full counsel of God because He accepted the wisdom of His Father and He trusted fully in the sovereignty of His Father's plan for His earthly ministry.

While many Evangelicals will readily be familiar with the biblical passage that begins this introduction virtually no one will recognize the name *Susie Kyles* who I choose to attribute the second quote that begins this chapter. I freely acknowledge the quote does not originate with Susie Kyles, but nonetheless, this quote has come to take up residence in my life because I would often hear my beloved grandmother state this expression so frequently when I was growing up. She would always make it in the context of *Church life*. If you have not noticed, Susie Kyles shares the same surname as this author. I have been blessed for all of my fifty-six years to be able to call her "grandma." I quote her as my tribute to the impact she has had on my spiritual formation as a believer in the truth claims of Jesus Christ of Nazareth. While possessing only minimal education and with no formal biblical training, she remains one of the wisest and most God-fearing women (I know, I know, who does not say that about their grandmother but grant me this indulgence) God has blessed me to know. As I read about the virtuous woman in Proverbs 31, it seems as if God had my grandmother in view as He moves Solomon to pen this wisdom book. My grandmother would express the quote, "a religion that can't take a lick, ain't worth a lick," whenever it was important to point out Christians should not be so timid and thin-skinned and wilt when confronted with opposition or adversity. The Bible admonishes Evangelicals not to display a spirit of fear but of power and a sound mind (2 Timothy 1:7). Consequently, instead of dodging the conversation, Evangelicals should find delight in taking the initiative and seeking to speak God's truth into *all areas* of life, be they areas of politics, sex, or religion, whatever they may be. When properly understood, there is to be no subject that is off-limits if my understanding of 2 Corinthians 10:5 is correct: *"We destroy argu-*

ments and every lofty opinion raised against the knowledge of God and take every thought captive to obey Christ."

Cognitive Dissonance

It is November 8, 2008, and it is a historic night, in not only American history but also world history. I was serving on active duty as an Army Officer in Washington, DC, and I was on medical leave, recuperating from a recent surgery, so I had no fears about rising early for work the next day, but frankly, I believe it would not have mattered if I did. I joined countless other African Americans in particular and most Americans in general by being keenly interested in the outcome of an election in which an African American was one of the candidates of the two major political powers in America. From a strictly ethnic basis, I must acknowledge a very real part of me being delighted in the historical nature of what the candidacy of Barack Obama posited for our country. A country with an embarrassing and despicable history of its treatment of citizens created in its Creator's Imago Dei. This same country actually had a person of African American heritage vying competitively for their land's highest political office.

Yet for all of its historical, racial, and cultural importance, I was equally profoundly saddened by the political candidacy and subsequent election of Barack Obama. I wanted so earnestly wanted to be part of this historical moment for African Americans. Yet, I believe the Bible constrains Evangelicals who seek to submit to a grounded biblical worldview from such political attachment. The African American Evangelical capitulation to the Moral Revolution placed me at direct odds with Barack Obama's election's euphoria. This radical embrace was not limited to African Americans exclusively as many other Americans in addition to international acclaim accompanied the occasion when Barack Obama became the first African American president in U.S. history.

On the one hand, this was a clear and unmistakable sign America had taken a giant leap forward. A day that Dr. Martin Luther King Jr. famously opined for during his speech in Washington in 1963 where he yearned for a day when Americans would judge the *Colored Man* primarily on his character and not on his skin color. On the other hand, this election was a capitulation to pragmatism on the part of African American Evangelicalism that I could not in good conscience be a part of, and I firmly believe in the final analysis sternly judged by the God of the Bible.

I am not naïve, so I am keenly aware of America's retched and often deplorable treatment of African Americans. I fully understand how the average African American citizen would feel justified in voting for a person of color. Honestly, thinking from a purely naturalistic point of view, I still share many of their same inklings. After so many years of being disenfranchised and marginalized, I can easily resonate with the political fervor and sense of "it is finally our time" so many African Americans still feel to this day. Yet as much as I wanted to participate in this movement, I could not, no, more precisely, *I would not* join this historical movement. I *would not* because I have an identity that transcends my ethnic identity. I do not classify or regard myself as an African American Evangelical. My identity is first and foremost, with no close second, is as an Evangelical African American. Some might feel it to be, but I do not believe this to be a case of schematic nitpicking, only intended to be restricted for abstract banter amongst the cultural elites.

It might be said we come into human existence, first, due to our natural birth. Still, for Evangelicals, it is our spiritual birth as committed disciples of Jesus Christ that should lay chief claim as to how we regard and govern ourselves. There should be no allegiance to the trend to regard our faith as a cultural association with a religious group of people. No, our fidelity to Jesus Christ should be our chief aim. As the Westminster Shorter Catechism says, our chief end in this life and the one to come is to *glorify God and enjoy Him forever.*

My befuddlement is how my fellow African American Evangelicals, to the alarming tune of 94 percent, could in good conscience vote for a political candidate who was and remains part of a political party that passionately and unapologetically advocates the moral positions they do. When you begin to look at the implications of such a high percentage (94), that means most African American

Evangelicals who voted that I know personally voted for President Obama. These are African American Evangelicals who are family members, African American Evangelicals I grew up worshipping with, African American Evangelicals I have sat in Bible studies alongside, prayed with and evangelized the lost together. Nine and one half of every ten African American Evangelicals choose to act in a manner I believe to be totally antithetical to the principles and values they would otherwise hold and ardently defend. We are reading the same Bible, yet I seem to be in the *vast minority* of African Americans Evangelicals who posit a different political engagement worldview. I must hasten as this point to emphasize this position in no way infers I believe the Republican Party is to be the bastion of virtue and without its own issues. I equally posit Caucasian Evangelicals have some explaining to do as well for their support of the candidacy of eventual President Donald Trump.

In fact, if God grants me the desired favor, I intend to write a companion piece expressing the same bewilderment as to how 84 percent of Caucasian Evangelicals chose to cast ballots for President Trump in 2016 considering if it would have been Democratic Presidential Candidate Hilary Clinton being considered with the baggage of candidate Trump her candidacy would have been eviscerated and skewered by many in the conservative contingent of the Republican Party. How what is good for the goose is not good for the gander boggles my mind.

Consequently, I say a *pox* on both of their heads (Republican and Democratic parties), but I have decided to first address the matter of African American Evangelical duplicity for a couple of reasons. First, there is the obvious chronological dimension (the election of President Obama preceded President Trump's election) but second, and more importantly, I am an African American. I believe it is vital to speak to my fellow countryman, similar to some of the same tribal reasons the Apostle Paul longed to see his fellow Israelite brethren come to trust Christ as their Savior (Romans 10). Initially, before the Israelites summarily rejected him, the Apostle Paul would first seek out his fellow Israelites before he ventured to preach to the Gentiles whenever he would enter a new city to preach the Gospel.

I believe I am in a position to speak in a manner a Caucasian Evangelical would never dare due to our highly charged racial climate. I acknowledge at the end of this quest; I will quite likely be *persona non grata* by both sides. Yet I have concluded the potential cost, if one could rightly call it that, is outweighed by the necessity of fidelity to my potentate, the Lord Jesus Christ. My conscience is held captive to the will of God, similar to Martin Luther's famous declaration at the *Diet of Worm*. I have decided to *lean forward* into this conversation because I believe it is how I can make a difference, not necessarily in some fairy-tale, romanticized manner, but I believe there are many African American Evangelicals who have not been properly taught and though they are accountable for their lack of understanding, if they were presented with the facts, would, Lord willing, adjust their way of thinking and proceed to act accordingly. At least that is my fervent hope, yet ultimate results are always best left to the sovereign will of God. The Bible teaches the people of God perish for lack of knowledge. It is conceivable if the people of God are exposed to the truth that some, certainly not all, will repent and turn from their wicked ways.

I also *lean forward,* realizing I am not held responsible for how people choose to respond. Pragmatism is a concept that I will continue to reject passionately, and I devote an entire chapter attempting to refute this antibiblical, philosophical approach convincingly.[3] One of my spiritual heroes, William Carey, illustrates most beautifully why Evangelicals must never allow pragmatism to govern their lives. Brother Carey was a British Christian missionary who developed a heart for the people of India. He journeyed there in 1793, despite encountering considerable skepticism and ridiculed by many of his contemporaries in England. Many of his peers did not believe a venture to India would work because it had not been successful in the past despite the promise of Holy Scripture if the people of God went to make disciples that Christ would be with them as indicated in the

---

[3] Pragmatism is the worldview which understands that what is proper is determined by what works. If a strategy does not work, then it is not understood to be valid. The proper Evangelical worldview is, "If it is true, it will work." The Evangelical worldview grants superiority to what is true, not what works.

Great Commission (Matthew 28). Carey spent his first seven years in India faithfully building relationships, but he garnered nary one convert. It is keenly pertinent to note that one of his children died during these first seven years, and equally tragic is his wife suffered a mental breakdown. These actions alone and these actions alone would have been enough for many to conclude this movement was certainly not of God because you see, pragmatism is built upon *what works* as opposed to *what is true*.

Yet Carey persisted because of his unwavering commitment to his belief that his calling, his purpose for which God placed him on the Earth, was to share the Good News of Jesus Christ to the desperately spiritually needy Indian people. As Paul Harvey was fond of saying, "Now we know the rest of the story." William Carey is revered today as the "father of modern missions." Yet, it is easy to gloss over the seven years Brother Carey experienced no fruit for his labor, and that reality was compounded by the mental instability of his wife and eventual death of his son. It would have been so easy to look at the *results* and conclude Carey's initial foray was a colossal failure, but the employment of critical thinking and the benefits of being well-grounded in the faith equip Evangelicals to understand and embrace the truth God requires Evangelical submission to what we understand God to be calling us to do. If God so desires the result to be dramatic and numerically significant like when Peter preached, and three thousand souls were saved in one day, then that is God's business. Yet the same level of expectation is imposed upon Evangelicals when God summons us to a task, and we do not initially or even when we ultimately do not see much fruit from our labors. I thank God that dear Brother Carey did not succumb to pragmaticism.

Evangelicals have tragically, unwittingly and in some cases wittingly, embraced pragmatism seemingly whole cloth. I truly believe such is to be the case for many of my Caucasian Evangelical brethren as well. It would seem many Caucasian Evangelicals have consciously decided that although Presidential Candidate Donald Trump was a severely flawed candidate; they were still so passionately against the candidacy of Democratic Presidential Candidate Hilary Clinton (which I understand and fully share their angst) because of her radical anti-God worldview they still felt the best action, the most *pragmatic action* was to cast their ballots for candidate Trump. They believed he would appoint conservative judges, that he would affirm the traditional Judeo-Christian understanding of marriage, and that he would push back against the transgender revolution. While these are all virtues I fully subscribe to and hold with equal passion with my fellow Caucasian Evangelicals, the pragmatic concern, as legitimate as that concern may be, cannot *trump* (pardon the pun) what Evangelicals understand to be "true."

Thus, I refuse to align myself with the candidacy (but not with the subsequent presidency) of Donald Trump.[4] But again, this book will deal principally with the subject of African American Evangelicals aligning themselves with the candidacies of Barack Obama and Hilary Rodman Clinton in particular, and the Democratic Party in general. I only refer to Caucasian Evangelicals and their alleged political duplicity here to illustrate how toxic pragmatism can, has been, and sadly continues to be for and to the Church.

I am a visual learner, so I want to use imagery found in the Bible to illustrate my thesis of something being weighed and found lacking or wanting with one of the most ominous occasions found in the Old Testament. I take this imagery directly from the Holy Writ when the Prophet Daniel recounts the story of King Belshazzar, who saw some writing on the wall of his palace. The writing, which none of the king's wise men could read or interpret, was inscribed: MENE, MENE, TEXEL, AND PARISIN. Daniel was able to provide the king with the interpretation, which was *"MENE, God has numbered the days of your kingdom and brought it to an end; TEKE, you have been weighed in the balances and found wanting. PERES, your kingdom is divided and given to the Medes and Persians"* (Daniel 5:4ff).

I am not attempting to forecast any particular *eschatological* destiny for African Americans other than I do not believe how many

---

4   What I mean is although I did not support the candidacy of Donald Trump once he, in fact, became POTUS then my conscience is held captive to the Word of God. That captivity enjoins me to pray for President Trump, hold him in the highest regard that is biblically permissible, and to submit to His authority willingly.

African Americans Evangelical currently practice their political theology bodes well for fidelity with Jesus Christ and His teaching.[5] As a result, as to the degree, I am rightly dividing the Holy Scriptures, African Americans have no exegetical or theological basis for expecting to continue to inherit the blessings of God, that if God *has not* already given the African American Evangelical community over to our own devices like God chose to do in Romans chapter 1. Failure to adhere to live in fidelity to God's revealed truth did not work for the Israelites in the Old Testament, and no right-thinking person should expect it would be any different from the people of God in the New Testament.

The subsequent chapters will address the following premises to support my thesis:

(1)   African Americans Evangelicals are weighed and found wanting because we embrace antinomianism.

(2)   African Americans Evangelicals are weighed and found wanting because we embrace individualism.

(3)   African Americans Evangelicals are weighed and found wanting because we embrace pragmatism.

(4)   African Americans Evangelicals are weighed and found wanting because we embrace emotionalism.

(5)   African Americans Evangelicals are weighed and found wanting because we embrace elitism.

(6)   African Americans Evangelicals are weighed and found wanting because we embrace parochialism.

The book will close with my recommendations on both the internal and external remedies I believe are graciously still available

---

[5]   Eschatology is the Biblical discipline of the "last days" that inaugurate the eternal reign of God. Eschatology attempts to harmonize how the Bible reveals how our current world comes to an end. It covers but is not limited to, subjects like the Rapture, the Seven Year Tribulation, the Millennium Kingdom, the Day of the Lord, the Battle of Armageddon. There is no consensus within the broader Christian community. I subscribe to the Pre-Tribulation Premillennialist doctrinal position.

to the African American Evangelical community. Yet it must be said time is fleeting; we are here one moment and can be gone the very next second, so there must be a sense of urgency attached to the matter as well.

But hope and optimism, that is the encouraging message I want readers to be able to leave with after digesting the contents of my observations and critiques. Like the Bible's metanarrative, *encouraging news* loses its luster unless there is a necessary antecedent that makes the encouraging news desirous and desperately necessary. Put differently, good news is not anything to be sought after if a person does not understand there is first bad news to overcome.

Yes, these are grave matters that I believe have grossly been perpetuated within the African American Evangelical community. Matters for which God has and will continue to hold African American Evangelicals responsible justly but matters for which there still remains time to repent and turn back to God (how much time no one knows, so there must be a sense of urgency). We must be reminded that it is not so much how one starts, but really what matters is how one finishes. I desire more keenly to *die well* than to merely *live well*. There is no record of the martyr Stephen, from the Acts of the Apostles, necessarily *living well* (in human terms), but there can be no dispute from the biblical record that he indeed *died well*. It is my prayer that God may grant every believer this privilege to *die well*.[6] One of the ways to that end is how we choose to interact with politics as these types of decisions affect so much of the human enterprise.

Will one be able to say as the Apostle Paul was able to say under the inspiration of the Holy Spirit? "I have fought the good fight, I have finished the race, I have kept the faith. Henceforth there is laid up for me the crown of righteousness, which the Lord, the righteous judge, will award to me on that day, and not only to me but also to all who have loved his appearing" (2 Tim. 4:7–8). That is

---

[6] Stephen is recorded in the Bible as the first martyr of the new Christian faith. While Stephen is being martyred, he asked God to forgive those who stoned him to death, "for they know not what they do."

what I attempt to do with this book. My chief aim is to provoke the reader who already has a saving relationship with Christ to desire earnestly to walk in lockstep with Christ's directives. I do not believe an African American Evangelical can do so by voting for candidates from the Democratic Party unless there is a dramatic change in the Democratic Party's worldview.

Now, with God's help, let me begin the pursuit of supporting my thesis that no African American Evangelical who desires to display fidelity to Christ and His Word will vote for any Democratic candidate *until* and *unless* the Democratic Party offers candidates consistent with the Judeo-Christian worldview. I believe the destiny of many within the African American Evangelical community hangs in the balance. I believe our collective political engagement has a direct correlation with many of the societal ills that befall our community. I believe there is a passage from the Old Testament that serves as a timely and much-needed elixir. It is from 2 Chronicles, chapter 7, verse 14: *"If my people who are called by my name, shall humble themselves, and pray, and seek my face, and turn from their wicked way; then will I hear from heaven, and will forgive their sin, and will hear their land."*

To the end that my contribution to the dialogue within the African American Evangelical community brings glory to God and edifies the body than whatever criticism or rejection I may experience will not compare to the blessings that await me for seeking to be a good and faithful exegete of the Word of God and wise heralder of God's truth. May I be found faithful toward that end. To the degree I am off base, my soul cries, "Lord, have mercy on me, a wretched sinner." Let this be the true heart of every true believer of the Lord Jesus Christ. One day each and every one of us will literally stand before God's presence and give an account for our stewardship of the gifts and talents so lavishly given to us to contribute to the Body of Christ. Thus, this is no small pedantic matter of little or no consequence. As a result, I attempt to write soberly and with tremendous fear and trembling as I am a product of our progenitor, Adam. I would be the first to confess I am a marred image of God that has blind spots like all of Adam's offspring.

Yet I write nonetheless as one who boldly approaches the throne of God because I am confidence I have God's mind in this matter. I can and surely am wrong in several other areas of theology, but I humbly do not feel this is one such area. All I ask is for a fair hearing, and then I leave the results up to a sovereign God who's perfect will is promised via the Holy Scriptures to be done on Earth as it is currently being done in heaven (Matthew 6:19).

How do I so confidently declare such to be the case? Well, I can only do so because God declares it to be the case in His Holy Writ, and that is well enough for my soul. I trust this confident is true of all who read this book and shares fidelity in my belief as an Evangelical sold out to all the Bible teaches and reveals. Everything that God ordained to be done in *time and space* before the creation of heaven and Earth, down to the most intricate detail, will be accomplished without fail or delay. That is why I write with such expectancy and desire to be excellent and precise. I write not to curry the favor of any mere mortal. I write as one who seeks to join the great fraternity of Christian thinkers and writers whose chief goal is to make Christ known and made much.

Now that I have shared some of the background to my reasoning behind attempting to write such a book and expressing my hope and dreams, let us now get after it and see if I can make the case. I will endeavor to do so, never attempting to attack any person's integrity or dignity. I will, when necessary, challenge ideas and ideologies I believe to be hostile to the Gospel. I write with the expressed goal of building up the Body of Christ, and while the emphasis in today's culture seems to be titled to relying purely on emotions and feelings I believe the most precious commodity an Evangelical has to offer humanity is truth. Truth, undergirded by love for sure but done with an unwavering and unapologetic commitment to truth.

Evangelicals owe nothing less to our ourselves, to our neighbors, especially the ones blinded and held captive in darkness, and Evangelicals owe it with fidelity to the One who declares He is the Way, the Truth and the Life. I know of no more noble pursuit given to the human experience. Although I understand I will not reach the impeccable standard of literary perfection, I hope my puny contribution is at least a step in the proper direction. Only God Himself and eternity await to render the final verdict. Until then, I press on seeking to include this book in my humble pursuit to finish my fourth quarter strong and hear Jesus Christ exclaim at the end of my journey, "Well done, Ricky! Well done!"

WEIGHED AND FOUND WANTING DUE TO ANTINOMIANISM

"For the invisible things of him from the creation of the world are clearly seen, being understood by the things that are made, even his eternal power and Godhead; **so that they are without excuse** Because that, when they knew God, they glorified him not as God, neither were thankful; but became vain in their imaginations, and their foolish heart was darkened." (Romans 1:20–21, emphasis mine)

Free from the law, oh blessed condition!
I can sin all I will and still have remission.
(Antinomian Hymn)

Antinomianism comes from two Greek words, *anti*, meaning "against,"; and *nomos*, meaning "law." Put simply, antinomianism means "against the law." Theologically, antinomianism is the belief that there are no moral laws God expects anyone, but especially Evangelicals, to obey.[7] Now, properly speaking, it is not my con-

---

[7] I prefer the term *Evangelical*, while understanding the moniker, *Christian*, is used more frequently. While any moniker can be co-opted and thus marginalized, I believe *Evangelical*, attempts to differentiate and classify a particular version of Christianity because of its distinctive markers. Historian David Bebbington notes these four markers: Conversionism, Activism, Biblicism, and Crucicentrism. See https://www.nae.net/what-is-an-evangelical/ for a fuller reading on the topic.

tention that African American Evangelicals are full-orbed antinominalists. I readily concede the average African American Evangelical would vehemently disavow any notion of embracing such a heretic doctrine. They would heartily affirm all the essential tenets of orthodox Evangelical doctrine. I know from the onset many will immediately take great offense at such a polemic accusation. One can reasonably question why I would choose to pursue this line of reasoning to begin the dialogue. I consciously understand such an alarming accusation is surely to evoke an almost reflex, emotional, defensive reaction. If such a charge were without merit, then it will just be part of the typical divisive dialogue we experience on an everyday basis in American public discourse. Yet if there is a genuine basis for this line of argumentation, then not only *should* the alarm be raised, it *must* be raised.

I believe desperate times necessitate desperate measures. Desperate times, due to the almost universal (94 percent for Barack Obama and 88 percent for Hilary Rodman Clinton) participation of African American Evangelicals voting for presidential candidates from the Democratic Party. Suppose the numbers were more evenly distributed amongst both Republican and Democratic candidates. In that case, although African American Evangelicals still voted for Democratic Party candidates while that would still be theologically problematic, one might be able to make the argument this is the type of doctrinal issue that sincere believers could *agree to disagree*. You would be able to witness cogent arguments being made in both directions like so many Evangelicals are able to do on many secondary issues like baptism, worship styles, mode of church government, etc., etc. Yet I humbly, but nonetheless staunchly, believe no one can, as it stands today, postulate biblical fidelity and vote for a Democratic candidate, especially at the national level. However, the same is beginning to take place at the state and local levels.

Desperate times dictate I utilize direct and alarming language to arrest the attention of my African American brethren. Jude, the brother of Jesus Christ, beautifully illustrates this concept in the epistle designated by his name. Jude used the imagery of *snatching* people from the fire. No one would gingerly or lackadaisically remove someone from a burning fire. I trust the reader to be able to visualize easily the fervor and aggressiveness that would be employed in such a frantic and potentially life-threatening situation. Even if the action demanded the potential rescuer to mistreat the victim, the reader would believe the *rough treatment* was justifiable because of the alternative: bodily harm or even death. I would submit any rational-thinking victim, regardless of the minor scrapes from the "rough" treatment, would be immensely grateful for the rescue attempt. I understand this and, all analogy breaks down at some point, but I am remaining hopeful some African American Evangelicals will come to appreciate my attempt at their rescue from the fire. Perhaps not immediately, maybe never, but it is this author's desperate hope minds and hearts will change as God grants repentance. God could do so dramatically and suddenly, or He could do so over time after a season of reflection, mediation and prayer.[8] Regardless of the speed of God's benevolence, my only aim is for God's covenant people to respond, however long it may take with life-transforming repentance. I may have expired long off the scene, but I stand rest assured by the testimony of Holy Scriptures my labor for the truth of God's Word is never a pursuit in vain (Mark 10:29–30).

I submit to the reader these are indeed desperate times because I believe African American Evangelical's political alignment with the Democratic Party has made African American Evangelicalism complicit in the slaughter of an estimated sixty-three million lives aborted in the womb since *Roe vs. Wade* became the Law of the Land in January 1973. I would similarly submit the African American Evangelical community must *own* their part in the facilitation of marriage transforming right before our very eyes in this generation. There is no escaping African American Evangelical support has contributed significantly to the seismic shift in our culture's rejection of gender identity solely determined by biological birth and their radical embrace of gender as a social construct not governed by the

---

[8] My ultimate trust rests in the sovereignty of God. God normally uses secondary means to achieve His aims so, while reflection, mediation, and prayer are means of grace, if transformation is to take place, it will be solely because of God's empowerment.

sovereign will of God. These are not pedantic issues like the preferred style of dress one embraces, or the music one favors, or what style of art one fancies. These are not cultural preferences *that do change* as people's tastes change over time. These issues are not ceremonial or civil in nature, like the Old Testament prohibition of wearing wool with cotton or eating shellfish. Yes, the Bible reveals these types of Laws (civil and ceremonial) *can and do* change over time, but the Law's moral dimensions are immutable (incapable of change). What was morally correct a thousand years ago is still true and binding on the human conscience today. Evangelicals passionately posit that even if the Lord were to tarry His coming for another thousand years, the moral laws would remain insoluble.

All true and committed Evangelicals rightfully cherish the biblical doctrine we are saved by faith and not by works (Ephesians 2:8–9). Jesus Christ triumphantly declared that whom He has set free is free indeed (John 8:36). The Bible promises each believer; there is no longer condemnation once they have placed their trust in Jesus Christ as their Lord and Savior (Romans 8:1). The Law is no longer able to *accuse* the Evangelical because of the victory Jesus Christ wrought on Calvary's Cross. Jesus Christ was able to exclaim, *"It is finished"* at Golgotha (John 19:30). Evangelicals correctly understand Christ fulfilled all the requirements of God the Father's righteous demand for holiness. Christ is the end of the Law (Romans 10:4), and for that, all Evangelicals should be eternally thankful. Yet two different things can constitute tension and still be true at the same time.

Yes, Evangelicals have been freed from the Law's bondage solely by Faith through Grace, yet it is still true believers still need adherence to the Law to function properly as Evangelicals.[9] Please note when I refer to "the Law" I am making specific reference to God's Moral Law as opposed to God's Civil and Ceremonial Law.[10] Though there is room for disagreement in understanding what role the Law

---

[9] While works have no place in justification, they become very prominent in our pursuit of sanctification.

[10] It is beyond the scope of this book to deal with all of the complexities of how The Law applies to Christian. I embrace the Dispensational view that Christians are to allow the New Testament to interpret what OT laws are applicable today.

has for the Evangelical in this current dispensation, I do not believe genuine Evangelicals can embrace Jesus Christ as *Savior* but not as their *Lord*. Thus, it matters how Evangelicals, of all persuasions, comport themselves in all dimensions of living. Though this book is focused specifically upon the political dimension, the orthodox Evangelical worldview would be applicable to all other dimensions of the human experience. As a result, we could apply this principle to whatever social or moral issues that would arise in the future. For instance, who would have thought in a short five-year period the moral pendulum would have swung so quickly on the question of the definition of marriage. Think back with me, when then-junior Illinois Senator Barack Obama ran for president in 2008, he decisively affirmed marriage was confined to a man and a woman. Yet for the 2012 presidential election, his position "evolved" to an embrace of same-sex marriage. As long as Jesus Christ tarries His coming, the Evangelical Church must remain vigilant in displaying biblical fidelity to whatever "new understanding" rears its head in the marketplace of ideas. Evangelicals are being woefully naïve if we do not understand the onslaught will only continue and likely increase in both quantity and quality. All one has to do is read the Book of Revelation to understand it is even there Satan unleashes his full arsenal of tricks to attempt to derail God's plan. Thankfully, most Evangelicals understand the Book of Revelation's central message to Evangelicals is "we win."

History has demonstrated whenever the Evangelical Church has taken a passive stance; we have lost public influence in the culture. This is consistent with the biblical admonition to serve as *light and as salt*. Jesus Christ declared during His famous Sermon on the Mount, *"Ye are the salt of the earth: but if salt has lost its savour wherewith shall it be salted? it is thenceforth good for nothing, but to be cast out, and to be trodden under foot of men"* (Matt. 5:13). I reject any notion God intended the voice of the Church to be silent on matters that pertain to life's essential questions. No, it is correct we do not live in

---

In other words, NT believers derive their instructions from the NT, principally from the Epistles.

a theocracy like the nation of Israel did in the Old Testament, but I believe one of the reasons believers do not go straight to heaven after their conversion is because God intends for Evangelicals to serve as His moral solvent in an unbelieving and preserve generation (Matthew 17:17). Society, sadly oftentimes rightly so, ridicules the Church because of our hypocritical nature, but one should shudder to think how lower our society would sink into the mire without the presence of the Evangelical on the Earth since the ascension of Jesus Christ. One only needs to understand the dire warning the Apostle Paul prophesied about God removing the Holy Spirit from the Earth (2 Thessalonians 2:6–9). When the Holy Spirit leaves, those Evangelicals who embrace a Dispensational understanding of Eschatology, believe God Raptures the Church at that time.[11] It is at that time, according to Dispensationalism, literally all *hell breaks loose* upon the Earth. One of the reasons things are not as bad as they could be is the Holy Spirit is presently restraining a tremendous amount of evil the Adversary desires to unleash, yet because the Church is still upon the Earth the Holy Spirit holds Satan at bay, to no small degree.

God commissioned Evangelicals to speak as God's prophetic voice not because of any inherent righteousness on our part. No, Evangelicals do so only because it is because we have become crucified with Christ. It is only to His Bride, Holy Spirit enabled, combined with Christ's own declaration that we would do even greater works than Him (John 14:12), that allow Evangelicals to turn the world upside down (Acts 17:6) when we live in a manner consistent with the Gospel. Yet it is equally true when we do not live in a man-

---

[11] The *Rapture* is a doctrinal position from some in Evangelicalism that believes Christ will come for the Church at some point before Christ unleashes His wrath upon unrepentant sinners. There are different understandings of the exact time period the Rapture will take place in God's unfolding plan of redemption. Some believe the *Rapture* will take place before the start of the Seven-Year Tribulation. Others think it will take place in the middle of the Tribulation. I personally hold the position the *Rapture* will take place before the Tribulation. Hence, I am a Pre-Tribulation Pre-Millennialist.

ner consistent with the Gospel that we become impotent and subject to the discipline of our Bridegroom, Jesus Christ of Nazareth.

I offer the Evangelical Church's response to the Civil Rights Movement as one negative example. When the Evangelical Church had an opportunity to lead the charge for justice for all many of the Evangelical Churches adopted a "hands-off" posture and when they did enter the public fray their response was tepid at best. One can vividly remember a letter a group of Evangelical ministers sent to Dr. Martin Luther King, imploring him not to *stir up* trouble when he was arrested in Birmingham, Alabama. I believe the more significant consideration should not have been the "trouble" Dr. King was allegedly stirring up but the racial injustice that was allowed to stand as the law of the land. Jesus Christ, the founder of the very religion these Caucasian ministers purported to represent, said, *"Woe unto you, scribes and Pharisees, hypocrites! for ye pay tithe of mint and anise and cummin, and have omitted the weightier matters of the law, judgment, mercy, and faith: these ought ye to have done, and not to leave the other undone" (Matt. 23:23).* It does one no any good whatsoever to sing about the "great by and by" on a Sunday morning yet not take the opportunity to positively impact the *by and by* Monday-Saturday when it is within our power to do so.

Evangelicals are not free to live as they want just because they embrace Christ as their Lord and Savior. It does matter what positions Evangelicals take on moral matters and not to take a position is just as bad and, probably on some level, worse than taking the wrong position. Evangelicals are not free to flippantly embrace the legalization of recreational marijuana, as one example, because of its temporal proximity, no matter how great the public groundswell becomes. Evangelicals are certainly not biblically free to accept the sexual revolutionaries' rejection of gender identity assigned according to biology. Biblically minded Evangelicals reject the secular belief that sexual identity is only a social construct because Evangelicals believe everything that exists in time and space God is the sovereign Creator's inscrutable choice and is part of His good order. Evangelicals believe it is only when we follow God's good order that society as a whole is able to experience what one of my favorite theologians, Dr. Albert Mohler, refers to as *"human flourishing."*[12]

If society is to thrive, i.e., *human flourishing*, and experience what our framers coined as, *"life, liberty and the pursuit of happiness."* I would submit it will only be possible if God is the chief object. If God is the chief object; then, the only objective means we have available to us as creatures able to understand and relate to Him would be by His own self-revelation. Evangelicals understand that God reveals Himself through three principal means: through nature, through His Word and most dramatically through the personage of Jesus Christ of Nazareth. Understandably, many in the secular culture reject this worldview but for someone claiming fidelity to orthodox Evangelicalism this worldview is a *sine qua non (absolute essential)*. This book intends to delve into my thesis of how African American Evangelicals are living inconsistently to God's revealed Word concerning their political engagement.

Thus, concerning their political engagement African American Evangelicals are not free to vote in any manner they see fit and still claim fidelity to orthodox Evangelicalism. Actions will always have consequences and theology will always matter. There is no escaping these two maxims. Every action any Evangelical takes will always be based on some theological principle, even when it is done without any conscious, deliberate contemplation. An action as mundane as stopping at a red light girds its basis in theological garb. Our sense of fairness in sporting events is undergirded by our theological underpinning or if in negative applications due to our embrace of faulty theology. Our innate sense to rescue a complete stranger found in a dangerous circumstance is an action we undertake because theology is always lurking, even when it is lurking in the background. An action as noble and gallant as the New York firefighters rushing headlong into the fires in the Twin Towers on 9-11 is impossible in

---

[12] I readily concede the issue of intersex individuals require great pastoral care and sensitivity. Intersex birth takes place because of The Fall. It should be noted the best estimates are 1.7% of births are classified as intersex. Justifying the legitimacy of God's design for gender binary is analogous to the number of people who seek abortion because of rape, incest and health to mother.

a naturalistic Darwinian worldview where it is postulated what rules are the survival of the fittest and every man for themselves.

Why is this so? Because God writes His Law within the human heart (this promise is directed to Gentiles as opposed to the Nation of Israel, who God physically gave the oracles of God: Romans 3:2), according to the Apostle Paul (Romans 2:15). Mankind awaits a future promise of God when He will void the necessity of human teachers to teach us His Law because God will write His Law upon our hearts (Jeremiah 31:31–34, Hebrews 10:16). I say, "lurking in the background" because we do a great job of suppressing the truth in unrighteousness (Romans 1:18).

Theologians believe the Law serves three purposes:

1) Serves as a mirror to point out God's understanding of what constitutes perfect righteousness and highlights man's inability to keep the Law perfectly. That is why there is no appreciation of the Good News unless there is a vivid presentation of the *Bad News*.

2) Civil use: to restrain evil. People tend to desire to avoid punishment.

3) Guide for believers: The Law provides an objective basis for believers to understand what pleases God.

I would submit all three dimensions of the Law remain in place for all Evangelicals today. Although the typical African American Evangelical would reflectively deny any association with antinomianism, the consequences of their political engagement leave them susceptible to the charge, nonetheless. One of my favorite theologians, the late John Gertsner, in an article for the ministry founded by the late Dr. R.C. Sproul, deals deftly with the subject when he writes,

> "We are dealing now with a group of people who, apart from this doctrine, are genuinely orthodox. They have no doubt whatever that justification is by faith alone. And when they speak of justification, they mean the remission of sins

RICKY V. KYLES SR., DEdMin.

by the shed blood of Jesus Christ, the incarnate second person of the Godhead, who was born of the Virgin Mary, fulfilled the law on our behalf, was delivered up for our offenses, and rose again bodily for our justification."

The doctrine Gerstner is referring to is the doctrine of justification, specifically what Gerstner referred to as the *antinomian view* of justification.[13] As I have previously stated, I have many family members who have been lifelong Democrats. Many of them still reside in Chicago, and I do not for one minute doubt that many, but certainly not all, genuinely and passionately love Jesus Christ with all of their hearts as enabled by the Holy Spirit, of course. I have attended several churches in the Chicagoland area whose ethnic make-up was predominately African Americans, and they have displayed complete orthodoxy in all of the significant issues that Gertsner raised yet, I cannot ignore that when it comes to the ballot box between 88 percent and 94 percent of African American Evangelicals vote for political candidates who supported all manner of abortions to include partial-birth abortions, the radical redefinition of marriage and the full embrace of the sexual revolution concerning gender identity.

Professor Gerstner recounts how he engaged in dialogue with one of the chief proponents of what is called "Free Grace." This branch of Evangelicalism rejects what is termed "Lordship salvation." The issue in the debate is whether one has to embrace Jesus Christ as both Lord and Savior to be regarded as an orthodox Evangelical. One side, advocated by Evangelicals such as the late R. C. Sproul, John MacArthur and Albert Mohler, espouse the Lordship Salvation

---

[13] The Evangelical understanding of justification is ta legal declaration in which God pardons the sinner of all his sins and accepts and accounts the sinner as righteous in His sight. Thus, God the Father declares the sinner as "not guilty." The Protestant view on justification is in stark opposition to the Roman Catholic doctrine, where justification is based on *infused* righteousness. Thus, the chasm between Evangelicalism and Roman Catholicism that still remains today.

position while Evangelicals such as Charles Ryrie, the late Norman Geisler, and Charles Stanley espouse the "Free Grace" position.

Professor Gerstner entered into an intramural dialogue with Professor Ryrie about his concerns about Ryrie's theological understanding of justification. Professor Ryrie sought to ensure Professor Gerstner of his rejection of any embrace of antinomianism, even going so far as to provide Professor Gerstner a copy of his book on Grace, where Professor Ryrie makes numerous references to the importance of the Law in the Christian life.

Yet despite Professor Ryrie's protest to the contrary, Professor Gerstner came to the conclusion based on his commitment to exegetical integrity Professor Ryrie's exposition left him no choice but to response in the following manner:

> I wrote him a five-page letter expressing my deep appreciation for the parts he had underlined. I told him that I understood why he felt those statements freed him from the charge of antinomianism. At the same time, I pointed out that they did not do that because, enthusiastic as he was, he did not make the works of obedience necessary. They were highly advisable and very profitable. They were still, after all Dr. Ryrie's statements orally and in writing, optional acts. He did not remove the "minus."

I believe it is vitally important, and illustrious of the thesis this book purports to posit is to point out what Ryrie is guilty of in particular and African American Evangelicals are guilty of in general is they both are attempting to live out their Christian experience in the following formulaic fashion:

Faith → Justification—Works

The proper relationship of faith and works is a question the Church has continually had to wrestle with throughout all of its history, and it is an issue that will not be conclusively settled anytime soon, if ever. Thus, this is an issue Evangelicals must continue to be willing to dialogue about because the danger is some people will remain convinced they genuinely possess salvation when in fact they are not. Consequently, this is not some inconsequential issue of little import; instead, for some, eternity literally hangs in the balance. Hence, my belief the necessity for a book such as this. I can think of no more of a grievous thought of someone incorrectly believing they are a genuine member of the body of Christ when they are, in fact, not. Unlike a movie where the director yells out, "cut" and reshoot the scene, once a human being takes their last breath, they step into eternity and await the judgment (Hebrews 9:27–28). Unlike the Roman Catholic eschatological understanding, Evangelicals posit the determination at death is not trifold: heaven, hell, or purgatory. The verdict at the time of death is only binary: heaven or hell.

I am literally frozen with fear of the thought of one of my loved ones or close friends standing before Christ only to hear Him state, *"I never knew you: depart from me, ye that work iniquity"* (Matthew 7:23). This dire and foreboding warning can only apply toward *professing believers* is without dispute, given the context. These are people who performed great works allegedly in the name and service of Jesus Christ. They include people who prophesied and cast out demons along with other miraculous works (Matthew 7:22). Yet Christ will nonetheless declare He *never* knew these people. When the Bible uses the word "knew" it speaks of an intimate redemptive relationship between God and redeemed humanity.

It is important to note regarding the rejection of Jesus Christ what will be lacking is solely an absence of genuine biblical faith. Biblical faith in the Work and Person of Jesus Christ is the only sufficient instrument available to remedy the enmity between God and man. Yet it is equally important to note that authentic biblical faith *necessarily* produces fruit. That is the whole thesis of James' treatment of the subject when he writes about faith being dead without works (James 2). Raw, naked faith does not profit anyone, because even the demons have faith (James 2:19). Yet despite postulating mere intellectual assent to the identity of Jesus Christ as God, these demons are still destined to eternal damnation.

If I was convinced my disagreement with my fellow African-American Evangelical brethren was confided to an issue that does not materially and substantially affect the Gospel, then I would gladly hold my tongue (or as the older saints would say, "I would gladly hold my mule") and accept that we would just *agree to disagree,* and then we all could go about our merry way. But I believe for many within the African American Evangelical community; the issue bears directly upon whether they possess genuine faith or not. To the degree, this belief is unwarranted or overstated then, may God have mercy upon my soul. Yet to the degree this belief is spot-on, then it is indeed a fearful thing to fall into the hands of the living God (Heb. 10:31).

Grounded Soteriological Footing

Works + Faith → Justification (Roman Catholic view)
Faith → Justification → Works (Orthodox Evangelical view)
Faith → Justification—Works (Antinomian *view*)

Of the three formulas listed above, the only orthodox view is the second one. Of course, this is a condensed formula, but for the sake of this conversation, it will serve the purpose. Much more can and has been said about topics like regeneration, repentance, and sanctification, but that would be beyond what is necessary to address my thesis.

The first formula is categorically rejected by knowledgeable Evangelicals. This contention is the basis of the theological chasm between Roman Catholicism and Protestantism. When I use the term *Evangelical,* I do so consciously identifying myself with those in the Protestants community who do not regard Roman Catholics as co-laborers in the Gospel. I would suspect the average African American Evangelical would not be able to articulate the discontinuity between the Protestant and Catholics adequately, but that is part of a larger problem affecting the entire Evangelical community. Suffice to say for this focused discussion most African American

Evangelicals do not consciously and actively espouse a faith + work soteriology (doctrine of salvation).[14]

The second formula is the orthodox understanding of salvation the Evangelical community postulates. While the possession of salvation is grounded solely in faith alone, works are nonetheless necessarily part of the equation. Works do not *flow to* salvation, but they do indeed *flow from* salvation. The instant God saves an individual; the Holy Spirit indwells them (1 Corinthians 12:13). Where before the unbeliever was in spiritual bondage to sin (Romans 6), they are now empowered by the very presence of the Holy Spirit to now live in accordance with God's holy standard. This empowerment covers every dimension of the human experience. Thus, the expectation is that genuine believers of Jesus Christ would experience and exhibit transformed thinking in all areas of life, to include political engagement. God commands Evangelicals to abstain from all appearance of evil (1 Thessalonians 5:22), to not be unequally yoked together with unbelievers (2 Corinthian 6:14), to abhor evil (Romans 12:9) and have no fellowship with the unfruitful works of darkness, but rather reprove them (Ephesians 5:11). These are just four biblical admonitions I was able to produce on a cursory reflection of the biblical expectations for proper stewardship for people to accurately represent the moniker *Evangelical* (though many others choose to use other terms like Christian or believer).

So in summary, Evangelicals, of all persuasions, are to *have no* association with evil, not even the mere appearance of evil is a legitimate option; they are to guard their relationships, so they *are not* in close fellowships with unbelievers; they are to detest evil, wherever and whenever it is found and they are to have no association with any works associated with darkness, but, instead, they are to publicly renounce them.[15] While I freely acknowledge I obey none of those four admonitions perfectly, I do attempt to obey them con-

---

[14] Merriam-Webster dictionary defines soteriology as theology dealing with salvation, especially as effected by Jesus Christ.

[15] The biblical commandment to not be unequally yoked is usually seen only as a forbearance against marriage when I would submit the forbearance is broader to include things such as entering into a business enterprise with unbelievers. I

sistently and in ever-increasing degrees of fidelity. I would hope the sheer weight of this line of argument will convince the reader there is something definitely eschew in the African-American Evangelical political engagement when 88–94 percent of them who choose to take advantage of their constitutional right to participate in the elections of governmental officials choose to vote for candidates who reject the Bible's clear teaching on life, marriage, and sexual identity.

It is under this rubric I turn to the third formula: Faith → Justification—Works. The most charitable parsing of this equation would leave the person with a wasted and empty Christian life, devoid of power and vitality. The grave danger is any life that is characterized by this formula; the assurance of salvation should be in serious doubt. The Apostle Peter conveys a solemn warning to the Church about judgment beginning with the church. He writes,

> For the time is come that judgment must begin at the house of God: and if *it* first *begin* at us, what shall the end *be* of them that obey not the gospel of God? And if the righteous be scarcely saved, where shall the ungodly and the sinner appear? (1 Peter 4:17–18, emphasis mine)

The Apostle Paul sounds an equally alarming warning to the Body of Christ. He speaks of the believers' work going through the fire of God's judgment. The Bible reveals these works as either gold, silver, or precious stones (good works) or wood, hay, and stubble (inadequate or insufficient works). The Apostle Paul writes,

> Now, if any man build upon this foundation gold, silver, precious stone, wood, hay, stubble. Every man's work shall be made manifest: for the day shall declare it, because it shall be revealed by fire; and the fire shall try every man's work of

---

believe entering into a political alliance is rightly included in the application of the admonition

> what sort it is. If any man's work abide which he
> hath built thereupon, he shall receive a reward. If
> any man's works shall be burned, he shall suffer
> loss: but he himself shall be saved; yet so as by
> fire. (1 Corinthians 3:12–15)

Remember, this is the best-case scenario. The person under consideration still makes it to heaven and that is clearly to be preferred than the horrific alternative: HELL. Yet the commonly expressed belief *as long as I make it* should be rejected with all the force Evangelicals can bring to bear in their theological understanding. Imagine for a moment, during this magnificent ceremony in heaven. All the redeemed stand before Christ and all the saints of the ages are gathered. We lay our crowns down in homage to our Lord and Savior (Revelations 5). Yet imagine as you stand with no crown(s) to offer in praise and demonstration of your profound gratitude to Christ. Grace that He sovereignly extended to you, but grace He did not sovereignly extend to others. Imagine, the Apostle Paul will be present in this august body of believers, so will the Apostle Peter. Maybe your pastor or the person who led you to Christ. There will be countless saints from every epoch of the Church's history, some we have read about and have greatly profited. Giants of the faith like Augustine, Wycliffe, Tyndale, Luther, Calvin, Wesley, all of them will presumably be present. They will be to your left, and they will be to your right; they will be in front and back of you. Yet you will stand amongst them *without* any credentials to validate your fidelity to Christ. Yes, the Evangelical enjoys the blessings of heaven, but the absence of crown(s) will demonstrably illustrate you lived out your Christian life of sanctification in a manner not in line with the Gospel (Galatians 2:14). While we are never to seek crowns or rewards for self-aggrandizement, we are nonetheless commanded to live in the pursuit of righteousness. The fact that God has graciously chosen to adorn our faithfulness with crowns is just another example of His lavishness upon us.

It should come as no surprise, but I readily concede I will not be able to stand shoulder to shoulder with the likes of some of the titans of the Bible like Brother Paul or Brothers Luther and Calvin as well as many of my contemporaries but I do aspire to be somewhere in the *team picture* (I don't care if it is far in the back) of those who have faithfully finished their race and kept their faith (2 Timothy 4:7). Consequently, I am attempting to bring my body into subjection so, I will not be disqualified from the prize (1 Corinthians 9:27). I realize my political engagement is part of that necessary subjection and surrender.

I fear many of my African American Evangelical brethren have disproportionally placed their emphasis on faith without the proper balance of works in their soteriological understanding. What I do with my political vote becomes as important as what I do with my body? What I think inevitably becomes what I believe. What I believe inevitably becomes what I support politically and become politically attached. It is not enough to say I love Jesus but do not do the things He commands (John 14:15). I was recently watching a TV program where family members repeatedly pointed to the Church attendance of their slain family member as evidence of their deceased family member's faith. While it was easy to lament the tragedy of the family's loss, it was equally lamentable how the family members rested their trust on something as uncertain as Church attendance to validate the authenticity of someone who claimed Christ as their Lord and Savior.

Going to Church on a regular basis, as one random example, is commendable and even commanded in Scripture (Hebrews 10:25) but Church attendance without the corresponding adherence to the commands found in the Bible do not ensure *rest in peace*. Let me again emphasize, because it is crucially important and cannot be stressed too often, we are not saved by works but, we are saved by a faith that *does work*. There is a profound disconnect somewhere when between 88 percent and 94 percent of any entity can act in a fashion that does not align with the expressed tenets that entity claims as its source of objective authority, i.e., the Bible.

In conclusion, I reiterate the Law is necessary, and it is good. It does not produce salvation, but it does flow from salvation. I concur with James when he offered the challenge that you show me your salvation by your faith, and I will show you my salvation by faith and works. So let us use politics as an example. Politically, I should be able to illustrate my fidelity to orthodox Evangelicalism by pointing to what I do support and what I do not support politically. I have no idea what is precisely in the mind of God concerning political issues like the proper taxation ideology, economics, or immigration. Granted, there are general principles that address every inch of life found in Holy Scriptures. Yet I humbly acknowledge there is no way to be certain if God favors President Reagan's *supply-side economics,* or does He endorse Forbes's flat tax proposal as the best economical means for human flourishing. But I am convinced, without a shadow of a doubt, of His expressed view on sex, marriage, and gender. So when I consider whom to vote for, especially in national elections, it becomes crystal clear in my mind, as presently constituted, my vote can never be aligned with the Democratic Party. Voting for a Democratic candidate does not necessarily mean or even imply every Evangelical who chooses to vote for a Democratic candidate is unregenerate, but I want to enter my voice into the conversation and ask boldly yet with fear and trembling: does voting for a Democratic candidate, as presently constituted, glorify God and advance the Kingdom or does it open Evangelicals up to God's divine judgment and His divine chastisement. Calvin keenly exclaimed, "When God wants to judge a nation, He gives them wicked rulers." I leave open the possibility God will continue to judge us (African American Evangelicals) by giving us wicked rulers because we are callously disregarding His call for righteousness. I agree with the late Dr. R. C. Sproul when he said the following Scripture gave him grave fears. The passage that Sproul fears is in the Fifth Chapter of Matthew's Gospel, verse 20, *"For I say unto you, That except your righteousness shall exceed the righteousness of the scribes and Pharisees, ye shall in no case enter into the kingdom of heaven"* (emphasis mine). Whatever this passage ultimately means is beyond the scope of this enterprise but pause and deep contemplation should be practiced by all God-fearing men and women when they do read or hear this passage. For all their deserved rebukes, the Scribes and Pharisees were very still pretty observant in practicing righteousness. Their transgressions were not grounded in a lack of moral fitness, their faults were *adding to* God's righteous requirements and making their additions equal to Holy Scripture and then insisting everyone else toe the line and adhere to their man-made traditions.

Let us not return to a bygone day when society measured true fidelity by adherence to a set of rules like dancing, card-playing, and drinking. That was the result of fundamentalist overemphasis on outward conformity. Equally crippling for the Evangelical Church would be a sense what we do does not matter because we have secured our get out of jail free card. I can think of no reality more frightening than some African American Evangelical believing they are saved, only to die in that mistaken state. If such were to happen, there is no recourse after they have made their transition. Theology does matter, and while some matters of theology are challenging to comprehend, that fully is not the case in all matters.

Politically, I keep coming back to the Big Three:

1) Life
2) Marriage
3) Gender

It is unmistakable there is an immense chasm between the Republican and Democratic Party. I vehemently disagree when I hear people attempt to muddy the waters and try to say things like "there are no differences between both parties; they both are corrupt." But even if one were to come to that conclusion and found both parties wanting, then I would recommend they do what I do when I come to the conclusion no candidate is morally acceptable from either party: either do not vote in that election or find a third-party candidate. I will have more to say in conclusion, but I am supremely confident if enough African American Evangelicals demanded more from the Democratic Party the Democratic Party would be forced to acquiesce. Again, more on that later.

WEIGHED AND FOUND WANTING DUE TO INDIVIDUALISM

> For none of us liveth to himself, and no man dieth to himself. For whether we live, we live unto the Lord; and whether we die, we die unto the Lord: whether we live therefore, or die, we are the Lord's. (Romans 14:6–7)

> In bourgeois society capital is independent and has individuality, while the living person is dependent and has no individuality. (Karl Marx)

Man is a social being and cannot live alone and, to maintain a peaceful community, you need to sacrifice your needs or move out of your comfort zone and help others who need your help. (Taken from the cons portion of article *Pros and Cons of Individualism.*[16])

This should serve as no shocking revelation, but African-American Evangelicals, like the majority of people, be they religious or secular, enthusiastically embrace the *age of individuality*. I want to interject very early in this chapter, the first malediction the Bible records was when God created Adam, and there was not found for him a suitable helpmate (Genesis 2:18). Up to this point, everything, without exception, was glorious in the sight of Almighty God. Each day at the end of His creative order, He pronounced *it was good.*

---

[16] Pro and Con. *Pros and Cons of Individualism.* November 3, 2018. https://www.prosancons.com/politics/pros-and-cons-of-individualism/. Accessed 6/19/2019.

He even concluded at the end of the sixth day, "it was very good." (Genesis 1:31).

When I was in college, I had the privilege of being accepted as a pledge into the first African American fraternity: Alpha Phi Alpha Fraternity Incorporated. One of our requirements while pledging was to learn and recite on demand the poem "Invictus" by William Ernest Henley. One of the more dramatic lines of this famous poem is

> It matters not how strait the gate,
> How charged with punishments the scroll,
> *I* am the *master* of my fate,
> *I* am the *captain* of my soul. (Emphasis mine)

Now, the big brothers really emphasized we were to recite the entire poem with a sense of dramatics and flair, but especially so with the last stanza: *I am the master of my fate. I am the captain of my soul.* I can still remember how I naively believed those theologically incorrect, man-glorifying declarations were positive attributes at that time. This pagan worldview empowered my reasoning that I could *really be somebody*. I erroneously believed the Bible taught that if I was able to put my mind to it, I could defeat any obstacle put in front of me. That was *my then,* and thankfully this is not *my now.* By God's grace when I was a child, I spoke as a child, but when I became a man, I put away childish thinking (1 Corinthians 13:11). Informed Evangelicals come to understand when a passage like Philippians 4:13 says, *"I can do all things through Christ who strengthens me"* it is not intended to teach the world is our oyster and we can master any things we set our minds to do.

No, all the Apostle Paul intended to teach in this frequently misinterpreted biblical passage was that Evangelicals can live victoriously if they have a little or if they have a lot. Because in both cases, the Sacred Scriptures empowers Evangelicals to humbly accept the biblical promise they will be enabled by the Holy Spirit to learn to master the art of contentment. As a result, as much as I might want, I will never become a world-class pianist, no matter how much I want or earnestly desire. The Book of Philippians is not teaching what the Army had as one of their slogans: *Be All You Can Be.* Sounds nice, but like the theological incorrect bumper sticker: *God said it, I Believe it, and that Settles It,* this sentiment qualifies for the classification as one of my former pastors would often say, "That dog won't hunt."

Society, to include many Evangelicals, seem to naively believe the ultimate question that confronts our culture is what is best for the individual. As I write this chapter the memories are still fresh in my mind of a professing Evangelical female in a debate on the Evangelical podcast *Unbelievable* repeatedly asserting her autonomy to decide what is best for her body as it pertains to the issue of abortion. Granted, she was British in her ethnicity and not African American. Still, she is a perfect illustration of the mindset it appears the vast majority of African American Evangelicals adopt as their worldview. When I was growing up, the Church taught me authentic Christianity were best understood using the following rubric:

1) Put God first.
2) Put others second.
3) Put self last.

It does not appear in actuality this motif is embraced by the typical African American Evangelical. I believe this rejection of a proper Evangelical worldview plays a significant part in how African American Evangelicals engage politically. I submit for the reader's consideration my thesis the majority of African-American Evangelicals who voted in the elections of 2008, 2012, and 2016 did not do so considering the mind of God first and his neighbor second but with a sense of doing what they believed to be right in their own eyes, much like the mass mayhem the Israelites displayed under the leadership of Joshua shortly after the death of their first leader Moses (Judges 21:25). It appears King Solomon was prophetically precise when he declared there is nothing new under the sun (Ecclesiastes 1:9). There may be slight variations and minor and subtle differences in how human depravity manifests itself but this generation is following the playbook of past generations.

If my surmise is correct, the results will always end in disaster. If one were to take a critical look at some of the social issues confronting the African American community, I would submit there is a direct correlation between our social ills and our political engagement. The African American Evangelical community is displaying the same sense of reckless individualism the Israelites displayed in the Old Testament. Tragically, unless there is corporate repentance, African Americans Evangelicals have no justifiable basis for any confidence their fate will be materially different for them in light of God's stern rebuke of the Nation of Israel in the Old Testament. The stakes are just that high.

So while the ills of the African American Evangelical community are but a microcosm of the larger society, I remind the reader I write seeking to speak primarily to the African American Evangelical community. I write with the expressed hope for repentance in anticipation of the 2020 national elections. If the political tide within the African American Evangelical community is to be reversed, even to the smallest degree, it happens providentially only when African American Evangelicals understand what it truly means to die to one's self, to crucify one's self, to pick up our individual crosses, and then to collectively follow Jesus Christ. Lest you believe it to be inconsistent with postulating African American Evangelicals concentrate on their *individual cross* while simultaneously embracing the sense of corporate accountability, the Bible present this same tension. The Apostle Paul proclaims,

> For as the body is one, and hath many members, and all the members of that one body, being many are one body; so also is Christ." For by one Spirit are we all baptized into one body, whether we be Jews or Gentiles, whether we be bond or free; and have been all made to drink into one Spirit. For the body is not one member, but many. (1 Corinthians 12:14)

Frankly, I admit I find it a bit dizzying to follow the mind of Apostle Paul completely in this discourse. Granted, some of that is due mainly to my lack of academic acumen, but that is beside the point. One second the Apostle Paul emphasizes on the *oneness* element, but in the very next breath, he makes emphasis about the *communal accountability* nature of the Evangelical community. He goes on to say in the book of Romans, *"For none of us liveth to himself, and no man dieth to himself"* (Romans 14:7). We cannot escape the biblical revelation what we do as individuals *dramatically* impact others. Imagine even when we die, we do not die unto ourselves. Try or hope as we might, we cannot escape this truth. What I *do* or what I *do not do* in the name of Evangelicalism affects the collective whole. If you are a professing Evangelical, what you do affects the entire *body*, irrespective of the action. Because it affects the *whole body*, it of necessity affects the entire *Body's* head: Jesus Christ. Either the 88–94 percent of African American Evangelicals, who continue to support the Democratic Party politically, have masterly solved the maze, and I am the one who has completely missed the memo, or the opposite is true. In the final analysis, it is just that simple; both sides cannot be correct. Both sides could be incorrect, and a third option can be demonstrated to be the accurate view, but I believe the matter will be determined to be either I am completely out to lunch, or it is the 88–94 percent who is out to lunch. Thankfully, only God has the final word in the matter.

Now, if the issue only indeed affected only 6–12 percent of African American Evangelicals then that would still be tragic (all biblical error is tragic) but comfortably in the realm of what is to be expected as we would never expect 100 percent biblical fidelity in any issue while living in a fallen world. If that 6–12 percent of a given demographic were faulty in their theological mooring, then there would be no case to be made for me writing this book and, indeed no claim to be made for anyone to take the time to read said book.

Oneness vs. Communal Accountability

This tension of what I will call *oneness* and *communal account-ability* goes back as far as Cain and Abel. Cain attempted in vain to mockingly ask the question: *"Am I my brother's keeper?"* (Genesis 4:9). God graciously warned Cain that sin lay at his door, and God went on to instruct Cain that he would have to master the sin that lay at Cain's door if Cain were to maintain communal peace with his brother, Abel. Tragically, the Bible reveals the outcome, Cain did not master the sin that laid at his door. The dilemma then is the same dilemma before Evangelicals today. The remedy available to us is the same remedy offered to Cain. One of the chief reasons God calls all Evangelicals to pursue individual righteousness is by doing so grants us the right to speak into the lives of our neighbors. God providentially provides the opportunity for His covenant people to secure and maintain the sense of community, to do what Voddie Baucham calls *expository apologetics.*[17] While it would beyond the scope of this book's thesis, I want to emphasize again one of the primary reasons Evangelicals do not immediately go to heaven after being converted is that God wants to use Evangelicals to disciple the nations. We are only able to disciple in the context of building relationships as masterly modeled by Jesus Christ with His twelve disciples.

That clearly was one of the primary missions for the nation of Israel. Note what the prophet Isaiah wrote, *"And he said, It is a light thing that thou shouldest be my servant to raise up the tribes of Jacob, and to restore the preserved of Israel: I will also give thee for a light to the Gentiles, that thou mayest be my salvation unto the end of the earth"* (Isaiah 49:6). We find the same type of mission given to the New Testament covenant people as Jesus Christ gives His final marching

---

[17] Pastor Voddie Baucham believes *expository apologetics* is the pursuit to equip all believers as opposed to only the professionals to advance the Gospel. Each believer is uniquely placed in the strategic position to reach those in their sphere of influence with the Gospel that the professional will never be afforded. As one example, Pastor Baucham writes, "Expository Apologetics"—the practice of answering objections with the power of God's Word—is for everyone.

orders before He departed after the resurrection. Evangelical refers to this event as "The Great Commission":

Go ye therefore, and teach all nations, baptizing them in the name of the Father, and of the Son, and of the Holy Ghost: Teaching them to observe all things whatsoever I have commanded you: and, lo, I am with you always, *even* unto the end of the world. Amen. (Matthew 28:19–20)

I take seriously Jesus Christ's commission to make disciples of all people. While I do not do so perfectly, I do seek to do so consistently, especially when I meet someone for the first time. One example that will always stay with me is when I was on active duty attending a short course with other Army officers. We had a free weekend between the course, so several of us decided to spend the weekend attending stock car races. Being the team player I seek to be when a part of a group I spent the entire weekend miserably baking in the hot sun, watching stock cars qualify for the championship race that would take place later in the day. One particular officer, who turned out to be the big race fan, and I seemed to bond (or so it appeared on the surface) so we gathered the next day (Sunday) to grab a bite to eat. Now, anytime I am meeting someone and believe I have *earned the right* to speak into their life I proactively seek the opportunity to interject Christ into the conversation. After *sensing* that opportunity, I proceeded to ask my new friend the diagnostic question many Evangelicals use to evangelize. I asked him, "If you were to die tonight and you stood before God, and He asked you why He should let you live with Him for eternity what would your response be?" To my dismay, my new friend did not directly answer my question with a satisfactory affirmative answer, nor did he respond with an unsatisfactory non-affirmative answer. Instead, he answered with a startling answer that he believed his faith to be a "private matter." Needless to say, the remainder of our short time together was strained to put it mildly.

This Army officer's reply was alarming because properly understood, there are no "secret agent" Evangelicals. The Bible posits no one lights a candle and puts it under a bushel. A city that is set on a hill cannot be hid (Matthew 5:14–15). We are saved in this present *dispensation* because God has birthed an organism called the Church, made of Jews and Gentiles in equal standing before God. One of the first necessary requirements as part of the salvation process is to confess with our mouths that Jesus Christ is both Savior and Lord (Romans 10). This individualistic privatization of faith is yet another self-inflicted wound perpetuated within the Body of Christ. Our conversion to Jesus Christ is supposed to serve as a soothing solvent to the toxicity of this fallen world. The Holy Writ commands Evangelicals to be light for those hopelessly and radically trapped in darkness. It is one thing if this attitude is foisted upon Evangelicals by an ever-increasing hostile secular culture, but it is an altogether different animal if it is self-generated through either ignorance or, even worse, cowardice or apathy from those *inside the wire*. It is reminiscent of C. S. Lewis's poignant description of Hell. He writes in his book *The Problem of Pain*, "The gates of hell are locked from the inside." Once again, it could be said we have found the enemy, and that is enemy is more times than not inside the camp vice outside the camp.

Cultural Trojan Horse

There is an equally debilitating, insipid rhetoric advanced by an ever-increasingly hostile secular culture upon the Evangelical Church. It is the seemingly innocuous but subtly venomous, secular view that Evangelicals are free to *worship*. While that sounds reasonable and extremely accommodating, it is really intended to silence Evangelicalism from the marketplace of ideas. What is meant by the freedom to *worship* is "you Evangelicals can believe whatever you choose to think as long as you confide those beliefs to your places of worship. Yet it is to have *no place* within the public fare."

Let me allow you to peer behind the curtain and see an example of this type of thinking play out in my own individual life. Charlize Theron made the news recently for her decision to affirm her son's decision to identify differently from his assigned gender. What made this revelation so startling and of particular interest to me was the child was three years old at the time. So aside from thumbing her nose at God's freedom to create as He sees fit, we have the perplexing issue of an adult believing a three-year-old possessed the requisite mental acumen to make such a life-altering decision that brazenly mocks God's creative decree. If one could ever rightly posit it is ever a sign of mental acumen to make such a life-altering decision that contradicts God's creative decree. I posted a reply on Facebook expressing my bewilderment that a parent would believe it would be appropriate to endorse their child's decision to self-identify in opposition to their gender at birth.

Please keep in mind this was not a case of someone prying into the Theron household's personal life. Ms. Theron voluntarily chose to make her declaration public. She entered her worldview in the public marketplace of ideas. That being the case, I entered my voice into that same discussion as is my right, and I believe it to be my duty as one of God's agents. While I believe my position is aligned with the mind of God concerning gender, how it is possible my position is not permissible and permitted to be voiced in the public square if we truly embrace and celebrate diversity and seek to practice tolerance within the culture.

Yet I was quickly and emphatically rebuked by someone on FB for having the temerity to weigh in with my opinion about someone else's life. As an aside, I was severely rebuked by someone who is a blood relative (first cousin) who is fully aware of my Evangelical worldview. What my first cousin was clearly communicating is it is fine for me to personally and individually believe *whatever it is* that I choose to believe, but that belief has no place or business making public judgment upon someone else. In essence, believe and worship however you see fit in your personal place of worship or your private home but do not dare bring it in for consideration into the public fare. Affirming and celebrating the worldview of Thereon is perfectly acceptable and to be celebrated. Yet, if someone dares to interject an Evangelical worldview into the conversation, then there is no place for tolerance whatsoever.

Alarmingly, it seems more and more Evangelicals are adopting this as the accepted practice. In yet another example of Evangelicals' capitulation to the culture, the predominant issue is not a case of *outsiders* attempting to stifle the Evangelical voice, but it is altogether different and, frankly baffling, the issue is *insiders* acquiescing to confiding their theological beliefs within their places of worship. Whereas our spiritual *Commander-in-Chief* commands Evangelicals to comb the highways and hedges and compel them to come in and fill the house of God, many in the Evangelical seem content to gleefully hold their holy huddles (Luke 14:23).

God saves Evangelicals to serve as God's *visual aids* to a waiting and watching world. God does not save Evangelicals to pursue individual pursuits or for purely solely personal interactions with God. I believe it is important to note at this junction; there is nothing inherently faulty with pursuing individual pursuits with God. Again, this is one of those situations where it is certainly not a case of one versus the other; it is not a case of *either/or*. There will be times when it is wholly appropriate to focus on oneself. One of the popular refrains in the Evangelical Church is still "it is me; it is me, oh Lord, standing in the need of prayer. Not my momma, not my brother, not my sister, standing in the need of prayer."

It is a false assumption Evangelicals are never to think or be primarily concerned about themselves. While I believe many have not given the thought much consideration, think for a moment about being involved in a dire situation of some duration. What good would you be to others if you did not make a concerted effort to *first* take care of yourself? It is akin to the instructions we receive on airplane takeoffs. In an emergency, we are instructed to secure our mask *first* and *then* assist anyone else needing assistance. Evangelicals are never told in Holy Scriptures only to regard the interest of others. Instead, God commands Evangelicals to *"Look not every man on his own things, but every man also on the things of others"* (Philippians 2:4). That simple word *also* makes all the difference in the world. It means *in addition to*, so that would mean the necessary inference is the individual would have to look after their own interest as well as the interest of the other person, so it is clearly a case of *both/and*, it is not *either/or*.

If one were to really think about it for a minute, one could really come to see that life would not be feasibly practical if humans were never morally permitted or expected to place themselves first ever. I would not be married to my wife, Monique, if I felt I was obligated to give way to the *other guy* who wanted to pursue her. The present job I enjoy there were at least six other guys present on the day of my interview. I could not afford a case of *false piety*, so I knew I had to make the compelling (I would hope that is what it was) case of why they needed to choose me and not the other guys.

God saves the Evangelical to serve as ambassadors, as signposts to those wandering in the wilderness. There is a beautiful but yet elusive majesty in that God reveals Himself to be One, yet Triune, and this attribute has been eternally realized amongst the Persons of the Godhead. For all of eternity, there has been a Father, a Son, and the Holy Spirit. Three Persons but yet only One God. Profound and definitely beyond full comprehension. I believe both in this world and still indescribable even in the next.

Greg Gilbert elucidates this concept masterly in his book, *What is the Gospels*. He writes:

> The church is the arena which God has chosen, above all to showcase his wisdom and the glory of the gospel. As many have put it before, the church is the outpost of God's kingdom in this world. It's not correct to say that the church *is* the kingdom of God. As we've seen, there's much more to the kingdom than that. But it *is* right to say that the church is where we *see* the kingdom of God manifested in this age. (Emphasis author's)

Complexity of Individuality

The Bible is replete with paradoxes, both in the Old Testament and the New Testament. We will only be at our strongest by being aware and then acknowledging our weakness (2 Corinthians 12:8–10). The Bible reveals Evangelicals truly become rich by first becoming poor (Matthew 5:3). If we desire to lead, we can only effectively do so by serving (Matthew 20:26, Mark 9:35). We demonstrate Godly wisdom by accepting foolish concepts (1 Corinthians 1:27). Another one of those paradoxes is although every man only pays for his own sin the effects of his transgression are still absorbed by others, even according to the Bible to the third and fourth generations.

All one has to do is read passages like Deuteronomy 24:16, *"The fathers shall not be put to death for the children, neither shall the children be put to death for the fathers: every man shall be put to death for his own sin"* or Jeremiah 31:10 when it says, *"But every one shall die for his own iniquity: every man that eateth the sour grape, his teeth shall be set on edge."* It is even more explicit in Ezekiel 18:20 when God inspired Ezekiel to write,

> The soul that sinneth, it shall die. The son shall not bear the iniquity of the father, neither shall the father bear the iniquity of the son: the righteousness of the righteous shall be upon him, and the wickedness of the wicked shall be upon him.

It should be clear the Bible reveals I am only personally responsible and duly accountable for the actual sins I commit, either through commission or omission, in time and space. Conversely, the *righteousness* I perform God credits it to my account.[18] So far, so good one, would think. That would seem to be a principle right out of the Western worldview playbook. I make it or fail based on my own contribution. But not so fast; the Bible has more to say about the matter. It also says concerning this matter that

---

[18] My righteousness is what Martin Luther understood as an *alien righteousness* because the righteousness I perform is never done due to any inherent good on my part. Evangelicals do acts of righteousness only due to the enabling grace of the Holy Spirit. It is why the Apostle Paul wrote, "I am crucified with Christ: nevertheless, I live; yet not I, but Christ liveth in me: and the life which I now live in the flesh I live by the faith of the Son of God, who loved me and gave himself for me." (Galatians 2:20

> Thou shalt not bow down thyself unto them,
> nor serve them; for I, the LORD thy God, am a
> jealous God, visiting the iniquity of the fathers
> upon the children unto the third and fourth gen-
> eration of them that hate Me. (Deuteronomy
> 5:9)

One set of passages indicate children do not bear the iniquity of their fathers. Still, the passage in Deuteronomy 5 reveals the iniquity of the fathers are *visited* upon the children unto the third and fourth generations. What is the concerned Bible reader to do with these two seemingly contradictory passages? They are to understand the difference between direct culpability and indirect effect. While we will give an accounting for our individual transgressions, the punishment meted out to us will *necessarily* often affect others. Remember that is the point behind a passage such as *we do not live or die unto ourselves* (Romans 14:7). As a father, if God were to judge me for some transgression in a financial manner, would that not also affect the members of my household? Could that not also have a trickle-down effect on my grandkids, my great-grandkids, and according to the Bible, even to my great-grandkids?

Hopefully, it becomes clear how that realization plays into our discussion about African American political engagement? The political decisions we make in this present generation are directly a response to the issues that lay directly at our door. We can master it, or we can allow it to master us. The sin or righteousness is ours and ours alone to decide. Unlike the public debt, we pass off to our children the sin or righteousness associated with our political engagement is focused on us alone. Yet, we still have to be aware of the effects of our political actions will be realized by subsequent generations. The decisions of any administration will be felt for years long after that administration has faded from public view. Whether it be a president's Supreme Court nomination, a law ruled unconstitutional by the Supreme Court, or a law like "Obamacare" enacted by Congress, there is a potentially long-lasting effect on the American way of life.

This is only looking at the matter in the horizontal plane. What about the spiritual dimension? Shouldn't our spiritual concerns easily trump our temporal earthly concerns? I mean, shouldn't they really as the temporal is concerned with seventy, eighty, or ninety years and in some cases like my dear grandmother approaching one hundred years? Yet, the spiritual directly impacts eternity. For some, that will mean a possible loss of rewards for poor stewardship, but even more, pressing for others, it will only validate salvation never took root in the first place. Dire, strident words employed to meet a dire, strident circumstance. We don't have time for mindless niceties or sentimental appeals to political correctness.

You might ask why the spiritual dimensions should hold sway over our earthly temporal concerns when the concerns are regarding crucial issues like the president appointing Jurists who are either literalists or having Supreme Court Justices who are proponents of judicial activism. We could have Congress finally deal once and for all on the country's definition of what constitutes marriage.[19] One can easily agree these are pressing issues but none of them singularly or even collectively approach the spiritual implications for Evangelicals as to how they participate in political life.

Yet it is still essential to recognize no matter how vital the question regarding involvement is in political life for Evangelicals the supreme question still remains: How many people does it take to elect a president in a country of over 300 million people? I will answer, without reservation or hesitation, the answer is "One." You see, the only vote that counts in any election is who does God cast His "vote." So while it is certainly true when you hear people say, "every single vote counts" (all you have to do is ask the citizens in

---

[19] A literate jurist is a person who adheres to the literal representation of a statement or law. A person who translates text literally. A literalist understands the text to be static, deriving its meaning from the original intent of the author. Evangelicalism, properly understood, is based on a literalistic view of Holy Scripture because they understand the author controls the meaning of the text as opposed to the reader. Nonliteral jurists believe the document, i.e., Constitution, law, is a living document, subject to the whims, discretion of the contemporary reader.

the state of Florida after the 2000 Bush vs. Gore election) the sobering and humbling reality still remains the only vote that ultimately counts is God. The Bible reveals God is the One who *"changeth the times and the seasons: he removeth kings, and setteth up kings: he giveth wisdom unto the wise, and knowledge to them that know understanding"* (Daniel 2:21).

Now, exactly how we come to understand the sovereignty of God and human action in political affairs are well beyond the scope of this enterprise. All Evangelicals know is individuals vote but Evangelicals also acknowledge that ultimately only one Person ultimately decides and that Person sits in Heaven above. Yet Evangelicals do not deny the reality that individuals do, in fact, enter the ballot box and vote. The candidate who obtains the largest share of individual citizens' votes win. Both realities are true: individuals vote, and they do matter. God votes, and His vote certainly and ultimately matters.

Why is this digression concerning human agency and God's sovereignty pertinent to the discussion, you might ask? You might remember the background story behind the nation of Israel desiring to have a king like the rest of their surrounding neighbors. Even though God had indicated to Moses, it would be part of His plan to one day provide a king to rule over them the nation of Israel clamored for a king *outside* the will of God (Deuteronomy 7). As part of God's permissive will God allowed the sinful desires of individuals in the nation of Israel to come to fruition. Like a wise parent attempting to teach a "life lesson" to their wayward children God instructed Israel's leader at the time (Samuel) to anoint a king. God even instructed this leader, the flabbergasted prophet Samuel, that these rebellious Israelites were, in fact, rejecting God and not Samuel.

I believe it is quite possible that God is doing the same thing to the African American community. God judged the nation of Israel for their insistence upon having their own way. He informed them their kings would take their best land and their best men and women for his own pleasures (Deuteronomy 7). Yet even with this divine warning there were still enough rebellious individuals who *united together* to develop a consensus to oppose (humanly speaking) God's timing for a king.[20]

It is interesting that it appears the level of unity determines the level of God's response. If the amount of individuals who unite together in opposition is limited in scope, then God summarily judges only those who rebel. I point to the rebellion of Achan who appeared to be the leader of a band of individuals who choose to disobey God's clear instructions to devote all of the material they encountered in war to destruction (Judge 7).

The example of Korah serves as another prime example (Number 16). Korah, along with two leaders of the Reubenite clan: Datan and Abiram recklessly chose to influence 250 other well-known (famous) leaders to oppose Moses' leadership. Demonstrating this was not a trite matter, take note of the forceful reaction of the Lord to these rebellious individuals:

> And the LORD spake unto Moses and unto Aaron, saying, separate yourselves from among this congregation, that I may consume them in a moment. And they fell upon their faces, and said, O God, the God of the spirits of all flesh, shall one man sin, and wilt thou be wroth with all the congregation? And the LORD spake unto Moses, saying, speak unto the congregation, saying, Get you up from about the tabernacle of Korah, Dathan, and Abiram. And Moses rose up and went unto Dathan and Abiram; and the elders of Israel followed him. And he spake unto the congregation, saying,... And it came to pass, as he had made an end of speaking all these words, that the ground clave asunder that was under

---

[20] The Bible clearly teaches no one can thwart the plan of God so even what may appear as an act of successful rebellion of still under the direct control and authority of God. See passages like Job 42:2, Isaiah 14:27, Isaiah 46:8–11, Proverbs 19:21, and Daniel 4:35 to name just a few of the applicable Bible verses.

them: And the earth opened her mouth, and swallowed them up, and their houses, and all the men that appertained unto Korah, and all their goods. They, and all that appertained to them, went down alive into the pit, and the earth closed upon them: and they perished from among the congregation. And all Israel that were round about them fled at the cry of them: for they said, Lest the earth swallow us up also. And there came out a fire from the LORD, and consumed the two hundred and fifty men that offered incense. (Numbers 16:20–35)

Thus, what do I believe to be the proper response to individuals living in clear opposition to God's explicit instructions? I believe it calls for separation, especially if the proper warnings and pleadings have been advanced (Titus 3:10). There is no neutrality in this matter. We either enter the ballot box aligning with God or we are not. I am not naively stating the political options are always clear and distinct. They most certainly are not in many cases. Yet the opposite is true as well. There are things Evangelical can learn to tolerate and there are matters that should be non-negotiable.

I was just discussing this very subject with a friend I have come to love and respect over the year, even though we disagree about so many of the central issues of life. He is Roman Catholic, and I am Protestant. He is liberal in every sense of the word while I am staunchly conservatives in almost all areas of life. So while it was not surprising I do want to highlight a recent discussion where he reiterated his beliefs that Evangelicals (that is not the word he used but for stylistic sake it is my preferred term) should not seek to become involved as politicians. He reached that conclusion (falsely, I would strenuously interject) because he believed politics necessitate compromise and compromise is antithetical to a proper Evangelical worldview.

I believe where my friend from the great state of Illinois errs is his failure to appreciate category distinctions. Evangelicals believe there are different categories of doctrines. Most would agree there are primary beliefs, there are secondary beliefs, and there are tertiary beliefs. Of course, concerning primary beliefs, we must have 100 percent solidarity, and when properly understood, that is precisely what we see in the Evangelical community. We agree completely on doctrines like the Virgin Deity, God's immutability, Christ's bodily resurrection, Christ's sinless perfection, to name just a few.

However, there are a plethora of doctrinal issues that Evangelicals can and do disagree that we believe are very important, so much so, that we might not be able to fellowship or worship together but would still regard one another as Brothers and Sisters in Christ. These types of issues would be doctrines like the mode of baptism, the legitimacy of sign—gifts like speaking in tongues and miracles and the role of Women in ministry.

Yet still, there are those issues that we can disagree and in the final analysis would not necessarily preclude us from worshipping or fellowshipping together. I attend a Church where we heartily worship together and there are differences of understanding on drinking, head covering for females, worship styles, and dress, for example.

So when one understands the necessity for category distinction we should be able to see that there are plenty of areas, even in theology, that Evangelical can and do compromise without impugning the enterprise. Evangelicals understand we see dimly through a glass and it will not be until we come to see Jesus Christ that we will finally see clearly (1 Corinthians 13:9–12). Thus, Evangelicals do not insist upon absolute theological certitude.

I mention all of this to lay the groundwork to reinforce one of my main points to support my thesis. There are clear issues in the political arena that impact our ability to align or demur. They are again: life, marriage, and gender. These are the bedrock, the non-negotiables, the *sine qua non* issues that there can be no wiggle room in the Evangelical community.

There are other issues which would justifiably fall into the secondary category. They are vitally important and have a great impact on human flourishing, but good men can disagree on the best means to achieving the goal. These are economical philosophies (flat-tax, trickle-down *Reaganomics*), environmental philosophies—off-shore drilling, global warming beliefs) and regulation approaches (more to keep companies honest and less because the belief is freedom is key to innovation).

At the end of the day we are expected to do as President Kennedy said during his inaugural address in 1961. He said, "Ask not what your country can do for you; ask what you can do for your country." The challenge for the Evangelical in 2020 is not what is in *my best interest, but* what is in the best interest of others as revealed by God, our creator. He has not spoken with a forked tongue concerning the big three: life, marriage, and gender—the essentials or the primary.

If all things are equal on that level, then we can rightly move to the secondary level. The problem for Evangelicals is the Democratic Party fails to such a degree that no Evangelical can biblically justify a political alliance. At least, that is the position I am advocating based on all the issues I am raising and will continue to rise in subsequent chapters.

WEIGHED AND FOUND WANTING DUE TO PRAGMATISM

> Finally, brethren, whatsoever things are true,
> whatsoever things *are* honest, whatsoever things
> *are* just, whatsoever things *are* pure, whatsoever
> things *are* lovely, whatsoever things *are* of good
> report; if *there be* any virtue, and if *there be* any
> praise, think on these things. (Philippians 4:8)

If Jimmy jumps off the roof does that means you will jump too. (Author ubiquitous)

I would imagine every child has at some point heard some variation of the expression "if 'so and so' does *fill in the blank* does that mean you will too" from their parents. The wisdom behind this ubiquitous statement is it should never matter how prevalent or popular the actions of another person we should have the good common sense to not commit whatever act, or more likely, infraction, they are presently engaging. For me, as a child, it was likely stated by one of my parents in response to me copying some action of my best friend, Arland Fanning. They were essentially saying I "knew" better but chose to act in a way contrary to that knowledge because of the benefit I naively believed was more important to me at the time. Thankfully, most of the times as a child, my lack of discernment did not concern matters of great significance, and over time, I was fortunate to be able to grow out of my dependence on being part one of the guys. I would imagine this is the common experience of most people. As we mature and develop a more refined sense of self, we are not so easily swayed. At least, that is the hope and expectations as young people move into adulthood.

Yet I would submit it appears such is not the case for the African American Evangelical community, at least as to how they engage politically. Gone are the days when doing the right thing "just because" is reason enough to justify the action. This way of thinking seems to be a relic of the distant past. This is especially troubling in the area of politics. Too many African Americans find it humorous, and a *badge of honor* they regard William Clinton as as the "first African American" president. What many in the African American community find humorous I find repulsive and insulting. If you are not quite aware, President Clinton earned this moniker primarily because he admitted to smoking marijuana while in college and had a well-known reputation for "stepping out on his wife." Yet despite this baggage, Democratic Presidential candidate, Bill Clinton, defeated an incumbent president who was at the helm when the US defeated Saddam Hussein and went on to be a two-term president. President Clinton left the White House as one of the most popular presidents in US history, even as he faced impeachment for actions related to his marital infidelity during his second term.

Fast forward to the presidency and subsequent legacy of Barack Obama. It seems an almost daily occurrence that I can scroll through Facebook and view some African American share or post media revealing polls that report many people view President Obama as one of the most admired presidents in US history. Granted, I see the same type of hubris for President Trump from Caucasian Evangelicals and I remind the reader that is why I plan to deal with that issue in my next volume, Lord willing. But for now, I will continue to focus on the African American Evangelical perspective.

For some of the same reasons, African American Evangelicals should have rejected the candidacy of William Clinton; they should have rejected the presidency of Barack Obama. Let me state from the outset Barack Obama possesses a tremendous number of positive attributes. He was the first African American president of the Harvard Law Review. He demonstrated exemplary *selfless service* when he forsook lucrative legal career opportunities to perform community service after graduation. He became the first male African American senator from my home state, the great state of Illinois. He executed an eight-year presidency with no major scandals, personally or politically (and that accomplishment is huge in any era and to be significantly commended). He seemingly has two well-adjusted daughters and the perfect political wife who possessed a tremendous pedigree in her own right.[21]

Despite recognizing all of these positives I nonetheless still regard from a theological perspective, Barack Obama has been one of the most morally destructive presidents in US history. It was during his presidency the redefinition of marriage took place. While officially, the Supreme Court executed this action, it is clear President Obama was in full agreement and facilitated the governmental involvement in getting the law reversed. Many historians regard President Obama as one of the most aggressive presidents in advancing the *pro-choice* agenda. There has been a seismic shift from the Clinton administration to the Obama administration. Regarding the topic of abortion, we have gone from Clinton's *safe, legal, and rare* to what one Catholic Cardinal termed as *dangerous, imposed, and frequent.*[22] It was President Obama whose administration authored the now-infamous *Dear Collegiate Letter.* For those who are not familiar with this issue, here is a little background:[23]

---

21 I take my cue from Dr. Albert Mohler, president of Southern Baptist Theological Seminary (SBTS). Despite being an avowed conservative, Dr. Mohler placed a full-page advertisement extolling many of the attributes I reference and asked God's blessings on President Obama's presidency in a local newspaper in Lexington, KY. This gracious act influenced my decision to attend SBTS, pursue, and eventually obtain my doctoral degree.

22 Quote was made by Cardinal Timothy Dolan, the archbishop of New York, in a Washington Examiner editorial, *From Safe, Legal and Rare to Dangerous, Imposed and Frequent, January 29, 2019.* https://www.washingtonexaminer.com/opinion/from-safe-legal-and-rare-to-dangerous-imposed-and-frequent

23 Genny Beemyn and Shane Windmeyer, Campus Pride, *The Dear Colleague Letter on Transgender Students: What You Need to Know. June 9, 2019.* https://www.campuspride.org/resources/the-dear-colleague-letter-on-transgender-students-what-you-need-to-know/

On May 13, 2016, the Departments of Education and Justice issued a *Dear Colleague* letter to clarify the rights of transgender students under Title IX of the *Education Amendments of 1972*. While the question of how society should properly apply Title IX to LGBTQ+ students is a continued subject of great debate, this was the first official legal, government-sanctioned document specifically addressing the role of Title IX in this regard.

The Dear Colleague letter explains that K-12 schools and colleges are required under Title IX to protect the rights of trans students by

- providing safe and nondiscriminatory environments;
- respecting students' chosen names and pronouns;
- ensuring the use of restrooms, locker rooms, and housing consistent with students' gender identities and providing gender-inclusive and/or private facilities;
- maintaining students' privacy on school records.

The letter also specifically states that schools/colleges must treat students in accordance with *their gender identity*, regardless of their gender presentation, whether they have seen a therapist or had a psychological diagnosis, whether they have begun to transition medically, how legal documents identify their gender, and objects from other students, parents, or community members.

The letter went on to inform any school who received federal funding they would be subject to the forfeiture of future funding if they were found to be in non-compliance. I draw your attention in case you missed it to the government's stated goal. *Schools/colleges must treat students in accordance with their gender identity, regardless of their gender presentation, whether they have seen a therapist or had a psychological diagnosis, whether they have begun to transition medically, how legal documents identify their gender, and objects from other students, parents, or community members.* Bottom-line, as long as the child, no matter how young, makes the declaration, the school is obligated to acquiesce to the child's demand.

So in recap of the presidency of Barack Obama, we have experienced the abrogation of traditional marriage, a most radical embrace of the pro-choice agenda, and an aggressive embrace of the LBGT movement. All of these momentous sea changes occurred within a mere eight-year period. Amazingly, what would have taken several decades, if not a century, to be experienced is being experienced in a span of less than a decade. There is every reason to believe future changes will take place just as fast and presumably take even less time.

Regarding politics, it is virtually impossible to be dogmatic about what is the mind of God is concerning the fine details of what should a nation's proper economic policy be. Sure, we can grasp the broad concepts like fairness and protection of the poor and protection of private property, but does God endorse a flat tax or trickle-down economics, I am certain no one can state dogmatically. Does God favor offshore drilling, or would He instead desire we protect the environment and thus refrain from doing so? On issues like these and many more good people of faith and even people of no faith (they cannot be excluded from the conversation) can come to different conclusions. Yet, I am relatively certain concerning the mind of God when it comes to issues like marriage, gender identification, and the sacredness of life from the cradle to the grave.[24]

By my count on these three crucial social and moral issues the presidency of Barack Obama fails miserably on all three counts, yet many African Americans I know (and I realize that is a small sample size but still indicative of the general mood as evidenced by many opinion polls) still to this day speak glowingly of President Obama's tenure in the Oval Office. Literally, just yesterday, as I write this chapter someone posted a meme on Facebook of a President Trump press conference where a Trump staffer held up a sign allegedly asking if anyone knew how to get in contact with President Obama. Funny? Yes, I admit it was hilarious and I totally understand it from one perspective. I believe one can fairly question many of the decisions of

---

[24] I readily acknowledge the issue of intersexuality is a vexing one that requires a great deal of pastoral care and sensitivity. But I also understand intersexuality is a very rare occurrence. The Bible speaks to the normative expectation and not the rare exception.

President Obama, but I do not believe anyone can dispute President Obama always carried himself in a manner where even his most staunch opponent had to acknowledge the President carried himself with a high degree of grace and elegance. The late Senator McClain gained my profound respect when during one of his rallies when running for president, he decisively rebuked one of his supporters who attempted to accuse President Obama of being a Muslim.

It is most unfortunate as part of the increasingly toxic culture that rears its ugly far too often; we often feel the need to demonize those with whom we disagree. That is why it is crucially important for Evangelicals not to fall prey to such devices. Evangelicals, more than any other demographic, are rightly held to a much higher standard. Far too often, I experience and witness people resorting to *ad hominem* attacks whenever someone has the temerity to disagree with something they said. I have resigned myself to the reality it is frankly not worth engaging with people when they express an opinion, no matter how outrageous or baseless their position may be. Just yesterday (March 20, 2020) someone posted on Facebook, in light of the COVID-19 situation that now is not the time *for religion* but for us to come together. I would, guess she meant "come together" in a secular, non-religious sense. My first reaction was to immediately reply to express my vehement opposition but quickly thought the better of it. I have been down that road often enough to know all too well that it was highly unlikely any positive would have come from engaging.

Someone I attended Church with years ago when I was living in Chicago posted her frustration with Evangelicals who chose to not attend church the previous Sunday. That would have been the Sunday, March 15, 2020, right before the tide turned in America with many Churches (like mine) deciding they would comply with the President's directive to not gather in sizes of more than ten people. I even prefaced my comments; I was only sharing my perspective on the matter and then went to counsel that granting liberty was the best course of action in this matter.[25] I believe it was best to

---

[25] Please note everything changed when the COVID-19 outbreak continued to grow in America, and many churches closed their door and went to virtual

leave the matter of whether to attend Church or not to the individual Evangelical's own conscience. Some Evangelicals would err on the side of caution and refrain from attending, and others would choose to attend. Yet, in all cases, it would be important no one side accuse the other side of anything nefarious in their decision-making. Unfortunately, I used the word "judgment" in my reply, which is something all people do whenever there are options, and you have to make an assessment. In the case of whether to attend Church in light of COVID-19, all parties are making judgments; there is no escaping that reality. There is gross misunderstanding regarding the intersection of judging and Evangelicalism. Evangelicals judge all the time, and that is wholly consistent with orthodox Evangelicalism. The Holy Writ never teaches against judging, per se. The Bible only teaches against hypocritical judgment. There is much more that one can say about this matter, but I would just direct the reader to a good commentary on passages like Matthew 7:1–5 and 1 Corinthians 5.

The person I was dialoguing with immediately took offense to my reply. The individual never took time to deal intellectually with my rationale; they only chose to respond defensively to my characterization of their "judging." Of course, the individual was judging; we cannot make assessments without judging. If I am single and there are two eligible females, and I make a decision to pursue one as opposed to the other guess what I have just done? If I am new to a city and there are a plethora of Churches that meet my requirements for membership, and I choose one as opposed to all the others that meet that requirement guess what I have done? Words like judgment and discrimination are things people do each and every day without hubris and malice. But, unfortunately we have allowed perfectly good words to be demonized where they are viewed as inherently negative or evil when they need not necessarily be so. They can be, but they are not necessarily, which is a huge difference. As happens

---

services after March 15. The interaction I am referring to take place while the situation was more fluid and parishioners were making individual decision to attend church or not. For instance, on March 15, 2020, my wife attended church. My daughter and I chose not to attend. That did not make my wife wrong and my daughter and I wrong.

far too often an opportunity to have a frank and honest dialogue about the merits and demerits of whether to attend Church while the COVID-19 issue is still in full swing is lost because we have lost the art of civility in public dialogue. So while I have strong opposition to the worldview of Barack Obama, I will not succumb to the vile practice of demonizing him and not recognizing the many positive virtues he continues to exhibit, even as a former president.

So yes, there was and still remains to this day much to commend about the manner that President Obama comported himself but that will never negate the fact I fervently believe his presidency did not align theologically with truth in matters that are clearly delineated in Holy Scriptures. However, even to this day, he retains almost universal approval and exuberant support from the African American community.

That type of unfettered approval, my friend, is squarely grounded in the anti-Evangelical philosophical framework of pragmatism. I am sure that are some who are not familiar with the term *pragmatism.* Pragmatism is a philosophical worldview that bases its test for truth on whether or not an idea "works." If a certain idea seems to correspond to reality, (i.e., it works), then that view is deemed to be true. On the other hand, if a certain idea does not seem to correspond (i.e., it does not work) to reality then that view must be false.[26]

On election night on November 4, 2008, when one of the major networks broadcasted a live feed from the historic African American Church, Ebenezer Baptist Church, in Atlanta, Georgia I would humbly submit that was not because biblical truth was being vindicated. What was being vindicated was pragmatism in full display for the entire world to imbibe, and imbibe they most certainly did. The American People elected Barak Obama with the direct contribution of overwhelming African American Evangelical support *in spite of* biblical truth, not because of it. While many at Ebenezer expressed elation with so many others all over America and the world, remember the footage of prominent African Americans like Oprah Winfrey

---

[26] Chaffey, Tim. "Why Pragmatism Does Not Work." *Midwest Apologetics,* 04/27/2005, www.midwestapologetics.org/articles/philosophy/pragmatism.htm.

and Jessie Jackson visibly emotional celebrating at Grant Park in President Obama's hometown of Chicago; all I could muster that historic night was profound sadness and lament.

I cannot, with an eye on biblical fidelity, reconcile these two concepts: voting for the candidacy of Barack Obama and living in harmony with the following admonition from the Apostle Paul to his young protégé Timothy found in 1 Timothy 3:15, *"But if I tarry too long, that thou mayest know how thou oughtest to behave thyself in the house of God, which is the church of the living God, the pillar and ground of truth"* (emphasis mine). The Gospel never calls the Church, the Bride of Christ, to engage in pragmaticism as a means to any ends, no matter how noble that end might be thought to be.

I really believe African American Evangelicals, almost without exception, have completely ignored how we are supposed to behave in front of a watching world. Granted, 1 Timothy 3:15 explicitly is concerned with how Evangelicals are to behave in the house of God, but I trust the sober reader understands what happens in the house of God has a direct bearing on what happens once the Evangelical leaves the house of God. Every dimension of the Evangelical life is understood to be under the rule and reign of Jesus Christ. I would most sincerely hope every sober thinking Evangelical would heartily agree with Abraham Kuyper when he said about the majestic rule of Jesus Christ, *"There is a not a square inch in the whole domain of our human existence over which Christ, who is Sovereign over all, does not cry, Mine!"* It should be without dispute that domain would include the ballot box.

Why do I make such a bold declaration? Because how we comport ourselves politically is under the exclusive sovereign domain of Jesus Christ of Nazareth and it matters greatly how and with whom Evangelicals align themselves politically. Just as much and maybe, even more how we align ourselves sexually. Lest you forget or not see the connection, I draw your attention to the words of the Apostle Paul, *"Know ye not that your bodies are the members of Christ? Shall I then take the members of Christ, and make them the members of an harlot? God forbid"* (1 Corinthians 6:16).

73

I would submit to the reader when Evangelicals enter the ballot box, they enter that ballot box, in a very meaningful sense, taking Christ with them. That is certainly the thrust of the Apostle Paul's argument concerning the Evangelical's sexual liaison with a harlot. If one goes on to read and follow the Apostle Paul line of argument, we understand since the Holy Spirit indwells the Evangelical which according to the Apostle Paul "is in you" when the Evangelical commits fornication, they include the Holy Spirit in that grievous act. Now, *fully understanding* all of this is above my pay grade, and I cannot fully explain or answer all of the possible questions that may arise, but this much I do fully understand. Because the authentic Evangelical has the Holy Spirit actually taking up residence in their body, we make the Holy Spirit party to whatever action we undertake. That is why the Holy Writ expressly warns Evangelicals not to grieve the Holy Spirit (Ephesians 4:30). Fellow Evangelicals, please take a moment to digest this truth. The Holy Spirit is a Person; He is not an impersonal force. He has all the characteristics of Personhood like the other two members of the Trinity. That means He possesses the attributes of emotions and thoughts like any other person. Just as when I receive good news about my Son, I am joyful, but equally, when I receive negative news, especially if the negative news is because of my son's volitional acts, it profoundly grieves me. Hopefully, this analogy helps to make the connection. What we do as Evangelicals impacts the disposition of the third member of the Trinity that takes up residence in the life of every born-again individual.

Thus, the Holy Spirit delights in the truth. Like the Father, there is no shadow of turning within Him (James 1:17). He is just like the Father; He is so holy His eyes are too pure to look on evil (Habakkuk 1:13). He is just like the Son; He will be with us until the end of the age (Ephesians 4:30). He is like both the Father and the Son; He is sanctified in truth (John 17). Whatever the Father and the Son possess, the Holy Spirit possess in full and equal measure. He is the agent who ensures the Church is able to reprove the world of sin, of righteousness and of judgment (John 16:8). God, the Son, is the sole reason God, the Father, ensures God, the Holy Spirit guides the Church into all truth. (John 16:13).

Yet my question is if all of these glorious promises are true (and I will go to the grave convinced that they are) I will go to my grave, failing to understand how my fellow African Americans Evangelical brethren can, in good conscience, continue to go into the ballot box and vote for Democratic Presidential candidates. I concentrate my focus in this book on the election of Barack Obama, but my lack of understanding is certainly not limited to him, as evidenced by African American Evangelical support for Hilary Rodman Clinton. I would submit a valid argument could be advanced that African American political support singly handily rescued the candidacy of Joseph Biden. Many pundits were beginning to write Vice President Biden's political epitaph before he was able to win the 2020 South Carolina Democratic primary. Biden's chief source of political rescue: overwhelming African American support. Almost overnight, Vice President Biden went from packing his political bags to go down in history as a three-time loser as a Democratic presidential hopeful to the likely presumptive candidate from the Democratic party for the 2020 presidential election. The informed political observant is aware, the initial Democratic front-runner, Pete Buttigieg quickly faded from the scene. Why? Miniscule support from African Americans, nationally the number never rose above two percent. Faced with that stark reality, Buttigieg wisely realized in his words, "there was no path to victory." I point this out to draw attention to the power and magnitude African Americans possess politically. My lament is while African Americans Evangelicals could be working toward the advancement of the kingdom as God's agents of salt and light, we are instead are either wittingly or unwittingly serving as the Adversary's agents of darkness. Strong words indeed, but again desperate times demand desperate measures and these are indeed desperate times for America in general and African American Evangelicals in particular.

As I bring this particular argument regarding pragmatism to a close, the only plausible answer I can arrive at is a wholesale embrace of pragmatism is not theologically tenable. I do not believe anyone can make a tenable defense for the employment of pragmatism by a fair and reasoned accounting of the relevant biblical facts. I would submit African American Evangelicals looked at the matter through a pragmatism prism and understood the political capital they could collectively muster would play a large role in providing Barack Obama the political capital he would need to win the presidency. They were certainly correct pragmatically but there were ethically, morally, and biblically grievously incorrect.

I believe African American Evangelicals have gained the world, but the price has been our collective souls. Some will accuse me of literary overreach with such a bodacious claim, but I must politely demur because I truly believe the cost is just that grave. Similarly, I know some will take grave offense, but I would trade these recent hollow political victories for a return to African American voter disenfranchisement in a heartbeat. Now, let me quickly say I truly desire we can have both (biblically aligned political victories and African American voter empowerment) But, I believe Evangelicals can *wear* voter disenfranchisement as a virtue but can never do so when we vote in such a manner that we grieve the Holy Spirit. A proper biblical anthropology does not teach that Evangelicals will always "win" in this life. Many Israelites lived their entire human pilgrimage as slaves in Egypt, but the Bible teaches that God heard their cries. Yet, for many, freedom never came, but that reality is not an indication they *lost.*

We are not allowed to draw false conclusions in this fashion: Person A is a slave, and Person B is a rich slave owner. The faulty worldview translates to God cursing Person A, and God blessing person B. Hopefully, you can see the error in this logic. A Pragmatic worldview results in a logically flawed syllogism. It could very well be that Person A is the one who is a child of God while the rich slaveowner is the individual destined to an eternity of hell and brimstone. All one has to do is read the story of Lazarus and the rich man (Luke 16). Though there is considerable dispute in the Evangelical community as to whether Luke 16 is a parable or reflects a true historical encounter the message from both understandings is still the same. Our circumstances (results) do not determine our standing with God (truth).

Challis goes on to share how he believes pragmatism has invaded every area of life. One of his most salient points is success is measured by what "works" rather than what God's word says is true.[27] African American Evangelicals are rightly frustrated by the racism and the many other *isms* that have marginalized African American existence in America, not just in politics but in all other areas of the human experience. I believe this to be a fair assessment, and I hope no sober reader would take exception to this conclusion. The dilemma becomes, at least for me, what is the proper solution to this malaise? Is it to turn to tactics we believe will give us the best chance for success (however that is defined) or is it remaining firmly committed to believing and only volitionally doing what we believe to be true? Concerning African American political engagement, is it aligning ourselves with candidates we believe give us the best chance of winning, is it aligning ourselves with candidates who will believe will do the most things that we believe will benefit us personally. It is here it should be interjected one of the main criticisms of President Barack Obama from those in the African American community was that he was not "black" enough. There were very prominent African Americans who vehemently criticized President Obama because they felt he did not do enough to advance the "Black Agenda."[28]

Would not a vigorous pursuit and commitment to truth *necessarily* entail what would delight God would also delight Evangelicals? Would not a vigorous pursuit and commitment to truth *necessarily* entail what *would not* delight God *would not* delight Evangelicals? Then, where does the breakdown lay? Well, it most certainly would not lay with God, so the only other player in this scenario would be the Evangelical. Now, let me emphasize Evangelicals, of all persuasions, can and do justifiably so, come to different landing spots on matters such as the what is proper immigration strategy, on environmental issues, regulation type issues, on many foreign policies type issue and economic issues. The Bible will never speak specifically to

---

27 Ibid.

28 Tavis Smalley and Dr. Cornel West voiced strenuous and strident opposition to President Obama's fiscal policy. They believed President Obama failed miserably in addressing Americans in poverty, particularly blacks. One NPR article depicted the duo as making "a traveling roadshow out of their roles as the loudest African-American critics of President Obama."

any of those issues and many others that we will have to navigate as a democratic republic. The Bible will provide principles to govern our thinking, to be sure, but no one can dogmatically claim to possess the mind of God on these types of matters.

Yet such is not the case on matters the Holy Scriptures speaks explicitly. These are matters Evangelicals hold as first-principle type matters. This same very Holy Spirit that Jesus Christ promises will lead us into all truth surely has clearly spoken about when life begins (Jeremiah 1). This same third person of the Trinity is surely grieved when what the Godhead has joined together in holy matrimony is being mocked and discarded on our watch (Matthew 19). This same Divine Person, whom the Apostle Peter expressly indicated was lied to in the Book of Acts (Acts 5), is intimately involved in the *"Male and female he created and blessed them, and called their name Adam, in the day when they were created"* (Genesis 5:2). Again, grieving the Holy Spirit is not some, small trite offense that one can push to the bottom of the pile. Both Ananias and Sapphira lost their lives on the same day for lying to the Holy Spirit (Acts 5). We should not reach the conclusion that because the divine response from heaven is not instant and swift as an indication that there remains no consequence for subsequent acts that offend the Holy Spirit. That should not tempt the Lord, thy God (Matthew 4:7).

So while I agree wholeheartedly with Challis and many others that pragmatism has invaded every area of life this author is specifically concerned with how pragmatism has invaded our lives in the African American Evangelical community concerning political matters. We will remain dead in the waters if we continue to believe the ends will justify the means.

Faced with the choices of

1) Having another African American in the White House, but compromising our African American Evangelical witness

or

2) African American Evangelicals maintaining their Evangelical witness *and never* having another African Amer-

ican in the White House that imbibes from the current Democratic playbook with overwhelming African American Evangelical support I will take the latter every day and *twice on Sundays* a hundred times out of a hundred without batting an eye.

In a way, pragmatism believes whoever possesses the most toys at the end wins. Evangelicalism, when properly understood and practiced, pushes back against such a notion. We do so because we take our cue from Jesus Christ. When did Jesus Christ express such a worldview? He did so when He told His disciples, *"You know that the rulers of the Gentiles lord it over them, and their high officials exercise authority over them. Not so with you. Instead, whoever wants to be great among you must be your **servant**"* (Matthew 20:25–26, emphasis mine).

Many in the African American Evangelical community seem to embrace the worldview that African Americans have "arrived" because we were able to have an African American take up residence in the White House. They believe the system truly "worked" but I believe when we went about in the manner that we did, the system actually became "broke." How can Evangelicals rejoice when our very political engagement grieves the Holy Spirit? How can someone with a straight face posit the Holy Spirit is rejoicing when a presidential candidate is elected who supports the killing of human life in the womb and will eventually go on to support the redefinition of marriage and the rejection of the gender binary identification.

I would simultaneously humbly yet boldly submit such cannot and is not the case. The God revealed in the Holy Writ hates abortion, hates the rejection of His design for holy matrimony, and He hates the rejection of His design for creating them male and female. Unless someone can demonstrate how my exegesis of these three issues is off base, then a political alignment with a political party that is in open opposition to these principles are not a party of truth. Pragmatic, to be sure, but never true. Thus, no Evangelical seeking to be committed to truth can and should align themselves with the Democratic Party as currently constituted.

WEIGHED AND FOUND WANTING DUE TO EMOTIONALISM

> And the spirits of the prophets are subject to the prophets. (1 Corinthians 14:32)

> Here then, is the real problem of our negligence. We fail in our duty to study God's Word not so much because it is difficult to understand, not so much because it is dull and boring, but because it is work. Our problem is not a lack of intelligence or lack of passion. Our problem is that we are lazy. (RC Sproul)

We exchange truth-driven, Spirit-filled love for God with a flimsy counterfeit—an emotional high that can never last. Rebekah Womble, blogger, *Wise in His Eyes.*

I shudder to imagine a worship experience devoid of passionate emotions. During Christ's *Triumphal Entry* into Jerusalem that began His passion week He exclaimed in response to the Pharisee's criticism to Christ's disciples' public outcries of worship, *"I tell you, if these were silent, the very stones would cry out"* (Luke 19:40). Emotions are proper and to be expected, there is nothing inherently negative with the concept of emotion, especially in the context of worshipping. It is yet another one of God's *good* provisions to His creation. It is the misuse, not use, this is becoming an ever-increasing epidemic within the Evangelical Church at large, but acutely so in the African

American Evangelical experience. I am sure some can raise objections that the issue is also present in other ethnicities but

1) I grew up in the African American worship experience, so I report as a first-hand eyewitness.
2) I am making the argument the African American worship has a direct bearing on how they chose to engage politically.

I freely acknowledge the following diatribe is purely antidotal but a prevalent banter I experienced growing up in the African American Evangelical Church. It was went something along these lines:

Person A: "Girl, how was church today?
Person B: "Girl, it was great."
Person A: "Oh, that is great. What did the preacher preach about?"
Person B: "Oh, girl, I can't remember but we sho had a great time of worship!"

Now, of course, I have taken some liberties here and used a female version of the exchange but, substitute terms like "brother" or "sister" or whatever you fancy, and it is easy to identify with what I am positing. I grant, on some level, looking back on childhood memories can be a positive, engaging endeavor. As I type, memories begin to flood my mind about Deacon Brinker and Sister Petty. I can still clearly see my late pastor, Reverend Willie L. Hudson, and remember one of his most well-known sermons, *Valley of Dry Bones: Can These Bones Live Again?* My mind meanders back to the sermon he preached at my mother's funeral. He drew an analogy of my mother to Martha from the New Testament story of Lazarus and her two sisters (Luke 10:38–42). Martha was keenly, but ultimately unwisely, concerned with crossing every "i" and dotting every "t." Mary deftly understood there would be times to *dot* and *cross* to her heart's content at other times, but when Jesus Christ, the very God of God, Light of Lights, shows up in your living room, then *everything* needs to stop, and all eyes need to be on Him. While at that time,

I did not fully appreciate it, I have since come to better understand how Reverend Hudson so aptly nailed it in understanding and sending my mother off to glory.

But forgive my digression looking back on my sappy memories so back to my antidotal story, I know many of the African American readers will easily remember a back and forth exchange very similar to a conversation like this. I have vivid memories growing up watching members of the choir *strut and prance* while *worshipping and getting the Holy Ghost* during the choir time but fast asleep by the time the preacher began to preach. Even as a young child, my three brothers and I knew there would be *holy hell* to pay if we were ever caught sleeping in Church. So being as children often are at that age, we would find the sermon boring or not able to hold our attention. Yet sleeping was *never* going to be a viable option for our physical well-being once we arrived home (if you know what I mean, and I think you most certainly do). It was so patently obvious for all to see, as in our Church culture, the choir would remain in the choir stand (which was located directly behind the pulpit), so it was unavoidable not to observe the choir members as the preacher delivered the Sunday morning sermon.

Tragically, far too often, members would depart the worship experience believing they have engaged in an authentic commune with God. They incorrectly thought He would regard their *worship* as a *sweet aroma* because the Holy Spirit impacted their hearts without having the requisite intellectual engagement as well. In simpler terms, they cherished "heart" over "head." As the Bible laments, they possessed a zeal for God but a zeal that is without knowledge (Romans 10:2). The result is a man-centric glorification that is antithetical to the expressed object of our worship: God!

It is essential to acknowledge and freely admit there is *much* to commend for African Americans' passionate embrace and employment of emotions. Emotions are defined as follows: "An experience or mental state characterized by a substantial degree of feeling and usually accompanied by motor expression often quite intense. Any of various complex reactions with both psychical and physical manifestations as fear, anger, love, and hate."[29]

I believe Dub McCish has grasped the concept succinctly when he writes:

> The Bible student immediately recognizes the validity of emotion in Christianity in such terms as joy, sorrow, fear, hate, love, and even anger. These all have their part in the thinking and behavior of Christians. Emotion is also related to such elements as sincerity and enthusiasm. However, another term in the definitions that catches our attention is "feelings." Surely, none can confuse with Christianity a religion which does not involve the feelings of the individual!
>
> The question, then, is not whether one's emotions ought to be involved in his life as a Christian, but to what degree should they be involved?[30]

Thus, the vexing dilemma is not the employment of emotions in the life of African American Evangelicals. On the contrary, because all other demographics that constitute the broader Evangelical community would do well to incorporate *more feelings* within their worship and liturgy. No one should embrace and triumph a dry orthodoxy, and that is far from my intent or desire. Ministers should not be literally putting members to sleep with their dull, stale expositions of Holy Scripture. If members find the sermon boring, then it should be *in spite of* and never *because of* the tepidness of the preacher. I believe it is most insightful when Dr. R. C. Sproul indicates the chief reason many people give for their lack of Church attendance is they

---

[29] Clyde M. Narramore, The Psychology of Counseling (Grand Rapids, MI: Zondervan Pub. House, 1961 reprint), p. 279.

[30] Dub McCish, Emotionalism vs. Scriptural Emotions, False Doctrines of Man, December 7, 201. Accessed 9 August 10, 2019. http://falsedoctrinesofman.com/?p=1342.

find church "boring."[31] So a complaint about emotionalism does not seek as a response to fewer emotions or no emotions with dry, stale, tepid worship.

No, the vexation is the issue of emotions versus emotionalism. *Webster's New Universal Unabridged Dictionary* defines emotionalism as *unwarranted expression or display of emotion,* as *an undue indulgence in or display of emotion.* Emotions are useful and necessary, so this is a case where we do not want to resort to *throwing the baby out with the bathwater.* No, the baby is precious, and the Church must be vigilant to safeguard the baby at all costs. The baby is a precious commodity that is a *sine qua non* for the continued source of the Church's ability to remain a vigorous organism as well as an organization. It is the dirty and polluting bathwater that Evangelicals must seek to rid the Body of Christ. This polluted water impedes the Church's ability to be presented to her groom (Jesus Christ) as a bride without spot or wrinkle (Ephesians 5:26).

Authentic Evangelical worship *inevitably and necessarily* translates into both Evangelical orthodoxy (right beliefs) and Evangelical orthopraxy (right practices). It is not enough to believe enough of the right things without the corresponding right actions. It is not a question of how *high* one "jumps and shouts" in Church on a Sunday morning. How *high* one walks once they land and walk throughout the week in holiness is the only thing that truly matters and is pleasing to God.

It would appear, to coin a very popular phrase: *All is not well in Denmark.*

African American Evangelicals have seemingly learned to master the ability to pass a theological exam when it comes to espousing the right answers to theological inquiries. Still, when it comes to the rubber meeting the crucible road of life, the vast majority falls woefully deficient in displaying biblical fidelity when they engage politically. What should be an occasion for celebration instead; serves as

---

[31] Sproul made the following statement in his book *The Holiness of God:* A recent survey of people who used to be church members revealed that the main reason they stopped going to church was that they found it boring. It is difficult for many people to find worship a thrilling and moving experience.

a cautionary tale that many within the African American Evangelical community will never realize places them in great peril concerning their relationship with the very God that purport to pledge fidelity. Anyone who possesses an enduring and lasting relationship with God is one whose total being is positively affected. It must touch their head, their heart, and their hands. It must be intellectual, emotive, and *it must necessarily be* volitional. Being an orthodox Evangelical entails more than possessing the ability to posit the right responses to an abstract exam. It must find its correspondence in actions lived out in real situations, not in the laboratory or merely academic circles.

Yet, I believe this seems to be just the case. As late as 2009, African American Evangelicals scored the highest among the four major ethnic groups within Evangelicals (Caucasians, African American, Hispanics, and Asians) in a Barna Group study that measured faith and behaviors. The study examined the religious beliefs and behaviors of the black population today and in comparison to fifteen years ago. It also contrasted the faith of African Americans to that of the US population as a whole.[32]

Belief	US	Blacks	Whites
The Bible is totally accurate in all of the principles it teaches	49%	66%	46%
Have personal responsibility to tell others your religious beliefs	34%	46%	32%
Your religious faith is very important in your life	72%	86%	70%
Satan/devil is not a living being but is a symbol of evil	39%	46%	38%
when He lived on earth, Jesus Christ did not commit sins	43%	54%	42%
Single, most important purpose of your life is to love God with all your heart, mind, strength and soul	66%	85%	63%
God is the all-powerful, all-knowing, perfect creator of the universe who rules the world today	70%	84%	69%
Your highest priority in your life these days is your faith	11%	18%	11%
Number of persons interviewed	**9232**	**1272**	**6038**

---

[32] https://www.barna.com/research/how-the-faith-of-african-americans-has-changed/, How the Faith of Africans-Americans Has Changed, July 27, 2009. Barna Group

On the one hand, African Americans Evangelicals, more than any afore-mentioned demographic, postulate their faith is essential in their lives. Still, that very same faith somehow inexplicably leads them to align themselves with political policies that are antithetical to orthodox Evangelicalism. In fact, if there were indeed a harmony of orthodoxy with orthopraxy, one would expect to see African American Evangelicals point the way for all other demographic within Evangelicalism in proper political acumen. Political acumen as defined in those areas where the Bible clearly speaks without a forked tongue: life, marriage, and gender. This trifecta is by far the most pressing moral and theological issues confronting this present generation. Spiritual warfare necessarily demands Evangelicals, of all persuasions, to face the actual, real-life enemy before them. We, regrettably, are not afforded the luxury of determining the battlefield that lays before us. During the 1970s, it was the fight for Inerrancy, during the sixteenth century, the issue was Soteriology (doctrine of salvation); during the fourth century, it was Christological in nature. None of these combatants requested the battle that arose during their lifetimes; the secular elites hoisted it upon them. History has favorably acquitted the men and women who courageously pushed back against the cultural tides of their day. Sadly, I do not believe historians, at least those rooted in a proper Evangelical worldview, will regard the present-day African American Evangelicals contribution in such a favorable light and, I would submit it would be an assessment duly assessed.

Worship as Entertainment

Unfortunately, it appears we live within a culture that has ceded to the cultural demand for *entertainment*. An entire book could be (and most certainly has) easily written on the over-emphasis upon entertainment in many of the youth ministries in the average Evangelical Church. This capitulation is a major reason many of our young people leave and enter the university setting, and eventually reject the faith they "claimed" to embrace while living at home with mom and dad. Studies have shown that somewhere between 60 percent and 80 percent of previously engaged Christian youth become disengaged with their faith as they transition into college."[33]

Evangelicals in general, but African American Evangelicals in particular, have given way to the notion that if the Church emphasized on doctrine that it would repel people. The seemingly ubiquitous cry from many is "we need to focus on having an experience with Jesus." No matter if this alleged experience is wholly foreign and inconsistent with the biblical revelation. *Feelings* are now the buzzword in much of contemporary Evangelical discourse. *I feel* rather than *I think* has replaced, I believe, as the correct jargon in Christendom. *What I feel* as opposed to *what I believe is* how many Evangelicals believe is the proper mode to communicate biblical information.

It matters not what is being communicated from the pulpit as long as the preacher does so in a charismatic manner. As an aside, I was startled to learn one of the arguably most important sermons in American history many believe to be Jonathan Edward's sermon *Sinners in the Hands of an Angry God*. Trusted theologians report that Edwards was interrupted many times during the sermon by people moaning and crying out, "What shall I do to be saved?" Although surprisingly, the sermon has received criticism by some as a classic example of an emotional appeal to avoid fire and brimstone, Edwards' words have endured and are still revered by many in the Evangelical community to this day. Edwards' sermon continues to be the leading example of a First Great Awakening sermon, and many still hold it in high esteem in religious and academic studies.[34] Yet here is the kicker: many report this sermon by Edwards was not presented in a highly charged manner or passionately delivered. Historians report that Edwards read the sermon with a manuscript in a low monotone voice. Yet, the response from the congregation that day was palatable. A large number of people fainted, and others believing firmly in God's divine presence became overcome by emotions.

---

[33] Campus Renewal announced in a "Campus Ministry Link" report published on its website.

[34] *Ostling, Richard (4 October 2003), "Theologian Still Relevant After 300 Years," Times Daily, Associated Press, retrieved 2013-01-04.*

So, what would be the takeaway from the recounting of this story? The takeaway, at least for me, is not that emotions are to be frowned upon or discouraged. My takeaway is sometimes God shows up in a quiet; still, voice; other times, He manifests Himself in a whirlwind, and yet sometimes God decrees to reveal Himself in dramatic ways such as an earthquake. The point is there is no need to only expect God to be present when emotions are high, and the air is charged. Sometimes God is mightily present in the solitude of the moment. In fact, some of my profound divine encounters have taken place, not with bravado and great fanfare. No, just the opposite; it frequently happens when I am alone, and I begin to contemplate and silently reflect on some thought or memory of just how good God has been to me and mines.

Just as I am writing this chapter, one of my Facebook friends who happens to be a preacher posted an entry that is likely part of God's marvelous providence as I pen this chapter. My fellow co-laborer in the Gospel posted, "Preaching is too important to be reduced to catchphrases and soundbites." Someone then replied to his post with this comment, "Amen. Pastor!" Yet, I believe this sentiment is one that most Evangelicals do not practice in any real, meaningful sense. Ask yourself, "Who are the popular ministers in the African American Evangelical community? The common denominator will be individuals with allegedly excellent oratory skills and magnetic personality. Names like T. D. Jakes, Creflo Dollar, Jesse Jackson, Al Sharpton, Eddie Long, Fred Price are names many would list if asked to name current great African American Evangelists. I would have none of them because souls are too important to devote time and energy following people who give only dispense stones when milk (initially needed for new believers) and meat (needed for ongoing sanctification) are essential to feed needy and malnourished souls.[35]

---

[35] There are countless and nameless African American pastors and evangelists putting in and doing the work each and every day. So I am thankful that God always ensures there is always a faithful remnant who are gloriously empowered not to bend the knee. Some national African Americans Evangelical names I could heartily recommend are Voddie Baucham Jr., H. B. Charles Jr., Thabiti Anyabwile and Tony Evans.

I like what the Apostle Paul said, *"And I, brethren, when I came to you, came not with excellency of speech or of wisdom, declaring unto you the testimony of God. For I determined not to know anything among you, save Jesus Christ, and him crucified"* (1 Corinthians 2:1–2). Please don't incorrectly assume when Paul made that declaration under the inspiration of the Holy Spirit that he did not possess the necessary intellectual acumen. Paul was well trained and highly educated. He goes on to say in his letter to the Church at Philippi:

> Though I might also have confidence in the flesh. If any other man thinketh that he hath whereof he might trust in the flesh, I more: Circumcised the eight day, of the stock of Israel, of the tribe of Benjamin, an Hebrew of the Hebrews; as touching the law, a Pharisee; Concerning zeal, persecuting the church; touching the righteousness which is in the law, blameless. (Philippians 3:4–5)

Yet we live in a time where the preacher can't draw a crowd if he is not considered to be eloquent and possesses the gift of gab. How many of you know precisely of what I speak? It does not matter so much the content of the preacher's elucidation as much as how masterly he can spin a yarn. The predominant concern becomes, "Can he captivate and maintain the allurement of the audience through the sheer force of his personality? That is what is in demand from search committees and Churches at large. Staying committed to communicating the pure text and nothing but the text without a heavy dose of skillful articulation, and you are left dangling by the wayside. You will not gather an audience; you will not be considered relevant or someone to be paid attention to or taken as a serious candidate.

Yet surprisingly, we will wonder why our Churches are so anemic and devoid of God's transforming power. It would seem that many Evangelicals naively believe their Church because they have the new glib preacher, is the new hot thing. It seems there is little tangible cognization that God promised long ago that He is not interested in mere external observances and conformity. All one has to do is open up the Bible and read from the Book of Isaiah. It is there that Isaiah writes, *"To what purpose is* the multitude of your sacrifices unto me? saith the LORD: I am full of the burnt offerings of rams, and the fat of fed beasts; and I delight not in the blood of bullocks, or of lambs, or of *the goats"* (Isaiah 1:11).

Similarly, one of the Minor Prophets weighed in when he wrote, *"I hate, I despise your feast days, and I will not smell in your solemn assemblies. Though ye offer me burnt offerings and your meat offerings, I will not accept them: neither will I regard the peace offerings of your fat beasts"* (Amos 5:22).[36] I challenge you, the reader, directly is your Church choir known for their personal piety and fidelity to marked sanctification? Is your pastor known as a sound, sober exegete of the Word of God or is he, and sadly for some Churches, is she, known for their charisma and dynamic personality?[37]

One of my favorite expressions is the definition of insanity is doing the same thing, yet expecting a different result. One of the colloquialisms we embraced in military jargon was the concept of *self-inflicted wounds.* Being shot by the enemy, while in some sense heroic and noble because one is willing to risk such because of love to country, is one thing, but when we shoot *ourselves,* there is no gallantry to be derived from such adverse action. I would submit it is this unwise course of action being perpetuated in the African American Evangelical community, not by the *fog of war* but by a sheer act of our own wills. If you can remember the opening scene of *Saving Private Ryan,* you will quickly see how easy it is to get off

---

[36] Prophets are considered Minor Prophets only because of the relative breadth in the length of their writing, not in the importance or significance of their revelations given to their audience.

[37] I make no apology for a fervent defense of complementarianism as opposed to egalitarianism. The former holds there is a stark difference in the roles for men and women in the home and the church, while egalitarians believe there are no such distinctions. Thus, women are biblically qualified to serve as pastors in the church and are able to teach and have authority over men. They believe women are equal stewards in both essence and function in the home. I might add this belief is practically and logically incoherent. In a two-party union, if both parties are equal in function what happens when there is a tie.

course during a fierce battle. Mayhem is happening all around you, and it is easy to become disoriented. When that happens, then bad things can and often do take place. But that is not what I believe is happening in the African American Evangelical Church, in large measures. Parodying the words of President Franklin D. Roosevelt: African American Evangelicals, we have found the enemy, and tragically, but wholly avoidable, the enemy is *us*.

It becomes a vicious cycle. The laity demands entertainment, so preachers, who desire to shepherd God's people, realize they have to give the people what they want if they want to remain employed and considered relevant. So not surprisingly, but poisonous, non-convictional preachers capitulate to the whims of the body.

The problem becomes the Adversary will *never* be satisfied with the status quo. He will always seek more and more. I draw your attention back to the three temptations in the wilderness. The temptations escalate in scale and culminate with Satan actually requesting that Jesus Christ bow down and worship him. It starts with a mere appeal to personal comfort (hunger), moves to safety, and ends with a request for worship (Matthew 4:1–11). It is like the adage, give an inch, then the desire becomes a foot. History reveals that was the tragic fault with Neville Chambers; he naively believed if he gave Hitler Czechoslovakia that his decision would achieve, in his words, "peace in our time." Well, even the casual observer of history knows all too well, such was not the case. Hitler went on to invade Poland a year later. Thank God for courageous men like Winston Churchill. Though flawed, like all mere mortals, Churchill, along with others to be sure, galvanized the world to stand up and fight, and eventually defeated Hitler and his satanically inspired desire for world dominion. Legendary General George S. Patton once allegedly said, "War is hell." While that is most certainly true, it is more regrettable to not directly and decisively confront evil when it rears its ugly head. Whether my fellow African American Evangelicals come to understand that is all I am trying to do, I will nonetheless press on and make my case.

Satan's assault often begins when spiritually lackadaisical and biblically malnourished Evangelicals open the door a crack; Satan sneaks his foot in so the door cannot be fully shut. He woos us with sweet nothings, with offers of earth-bound fruits, bidding his time, patiently waiting until he can ease more of himself in our home. Once in the house, he is content with even taking up residence in the basement for a time. Next thing you know, he is hanging out in the family room, and he becomes just one of the guys. His approach is rarely dramatic and aggressive; it is low-key and gradual over time. He is rarely, if ever, pushy, not usually attempting to make a frontal assault. That is not his *modus operandi* (method of operation). Instead, he typically employs a flanking action where the chink in our defenses is often the soft underbelly, susceptible to penetration.

Using one example, Satan has masterly introduced a concept, which many African American Evangelicals understand as whooping. Satan masterfully understands human psychology, not because he is omniscient "all-knowing" like God, but because he is like a roaring lion seeking whom he may devour (1 Peter 5:8).[38] As a young child, I fondly remember the nature show *Wild Kingdom*. It was this show that I learned about the wiles employed by lions when they hunt. They use the skill of observant to scout out the weakness of the herd. Once they identify the weakling, they wait patiently and attack at just the ideal time and place.

In the same manner, Satan has observed over time what stirs the emotions of people. People love someone with the skills of oratory. We gravitate to people who can make a visceral connection to our hearts. The Bible accurately prophesied there would be a great movement of professing Evangelicals who grievously crave emotional-based preaching. The Apostle Paul warned believers when he wrote, *"For the time will come when they will not endure sound doctrine; but after their lusts shall they heap to themselves teachers, having itching ears"* (2 Timothy 4:3).

Any aspiring theologian cannot speak too long or write too much without appealing to the late great theologian Dr. R. C. Sproul. I have benefitted greatly from Dr. Sproul's wise counsel, and this sub-

---

[38] Whooping is a celebratory style of black preaching that pastors typically use to close a sermon. Some church scholars compare it to opera; it's that moment the sermon segues into song.

ject will be no exception. I submit for your sober consideration what Dr. Sproul so eloquently contributes to the conversation:

> For the soul of a person to be inflamed with passion for the living God, that person's mind must *first* be informed about the character and will of God. There can be nothing in the heart that is not first in the mind. Though it is possible to have theology on the head without its piercing the soul, it cannot pierce the soul without first being grasped by the mind. (emphasis mine)

I readily acknowledge what I am about to posit will be vehemently denied and personally resented by many in the African American Evangelical community, but I submit many in the African American Evangelical community their interaction with Evangelicalism has not incorporated both the intellectual *and* the emotive aspects of faith. I know I have mentioned it before but indulge me because I think understanding this is instrumental if we are to see why *whooping* should be rejected and phased out of African American Evangelical life. Emotions are, to be celebrated, championed, and embraced to be sure. Still, it is utterly tragic; I can easily remember one of the most common conversations I would hear growing up would take place as follows:

Person A: "Boy, did we have church today!
Person B: "Oh, what did the preacher preached about?
Person A: "I couldn't tell you, but boy did we have some church today!

Researching the history of *whooping*, I am totally flabbergasted there is still an actual debate within the African American Evangelical community. I don't understand why Evangelicals still consider *whooping* a legitimate medium in the Church's pursuit of evangelism toward the unsaved and sanctification of the saints as they seek to grow in their faith. Hopefully, by now, it should not surprise anyone

I would agree with Teresa L. Fry Brown, Director of Black Church Studies at Emory University in Atlanta, when she writes,

> People use to scoff at the itinerant "jackleg" preachers in the 1940s and 1950s who whooped their way through empty sermons, making up texts. Preachers who give their congregation a whoop but no substance leave their parishioners with nothing to get them through the week, Brown says. "They deliver diabetic sermons. You have a shot of insulin, but you have to come back later," Brown says. "It's like a candy high. They never look at the text; never any substance. All they give you is sounds.[39]

Now, I acknowledge everyone in the African American Evangelical community does not share Brown's perspective. For instance, the Rev. E. Dewey Smith Jr, a featured panelist on a CNN Special hosted by Soledad O'Brien titled *Almighty Debt: A Black in America Special* said, "It's [whooping] is in the DNA of our people." Smith says, "When people were beaten and bruised, the slave preacher, with the intonation of the voice, was able to lift the spirits of the people." Smith went on to justify his use of *whooping* during the CNN broadcast because believed "he had already given his congregation the "meat" of his message: scriptural references, archaeological asides, modern application—all the fancy stuff he learned in seminary. Now he was about to give them the gravy. It was the time to "whoop."[40]

Here is my pushback. If *whooping* is a *sine qua non,* why do we not find any example of it in the Holy Scriptures? We most certainly have examples of preaching in the New Testament. We clearly have what is probably the greatest sermon delivered in time and space. Can anyone

---

[39] Blake, John. (2010) 'Whooping is the Soundtrack for the Black church experience', *Indianapolis Recorder,* 28 October. Available at http://www.indianapolisrecorder.com/religion/article_fcee1675-3ed9-5784-942c-e6e3045aa413.html (Accessed: 4 April, 2020).

[40] Ibid.

dispute the communicator of that sermon to be none other than Jesus Christ of Nazareth? Of course, the sermon I refer to is Christ's Sermon on the Mount. We find *The Sermon on the Mount* recorded in each of the Synoptics, yet we have no allusion to the employment of whooping or anything akin to such a practice. Not only do we have this example, but I believe one of Jesus Christ's first recorded exposition beautifully negates the need or even benefit of *whooping*. Recorded in Luke chapter 4, shortly after Christ's encounter with Satan and the three temptations, Jesus Christ returned to Galilee teaching in the synagogues in Nazareth (Christ's hometown). One particular Sabbath, Luke writes that Christ took the Book of Esaias and read from a passage found in Isaiah 61. He simply reads from the passage and quietly, without any fanfare, hands the book back to the minister.

Now, I grant there is a real sense everything Jesus Christ did during His first advent was *sui generis* (absolutely unique). Still, we deftly balance this belief with the theological understanding of *everything* Jesus Christ did in time and space was not sourced from His divine powers. Jesus Christ executed everything He did because the Holy Spirit empowered Him (Isaiah 11). Jesus Christ was the God-Man, and here we make special emphasis upon the human component. Many falsely believe Jesus Christ executed His ministry utilizing His deity, which the Holy Scriptures makes clear such was not the case. The author of Hebrews revealed, *"Forasmuch then as the children are partakers of flesh and blood, he [Christ] also himself likewise took part of the same; that through death he might destroy him that had the power of death, that is, the devil"* (Hebrews 2:14). I hope the inference is clear from this passage found in the Holy Writ, Jesus Christ had to take on humanity to become the genuine substitute for Adam and all of his posterity.

I would submit to you anything done in time and space that is edifying and promotes *human flourishing,* and if Jesus Christ endeavored, no one could do it any better. Jesus Christ endeavored in the art of preaching. Hence, He is the perfect illustration of what biblical preaching should properly look like. Any signs of *whooping? Anywhere? Anytime?*

Okay, I know some will accuse me of stacking the deck and not fighting fair by appealing to the ministry of Jesus Christ, so how about we look at, say the Apostle Paul or even the Apostle Peter.

Peter preached the first sermon that birthed the dawn of the Church Age as we know it (Acts 2). Of course, I wasn't there, but you best believe this was a sermon with plenty of emotion, passion, and vigor. Peter's discourse was not some stale, bland interchange, to be sure. Yet, as Don Cornelius of the famed TV show: *Soul Train* fame used to say, "you could bet your last bottom dollar" that Peter did not employ anything close to resembling the machinations associated with *whooping*.

God did not design worship so His creatures could properly regard it as boring or dull, nor is it when adequately understood. No fully mature Evangelical would advocate for a dissemination of cold, dispassionate orthodoxy. We must acknowledge some professing believers believe any signs of emotional response is out of place. There is even a biblical example of this erroneous thinking. I speak of one of King David's wife, Michal, when she attempted to rebuke King David for his, according to her, vile display of affections toward God. I really encourage you to read the full story but suffice to say David goes on to become one of the Bible's most significant and most cherished characters (2 Samuel 6). The record of Michal only reveals tragedy punctuated by barrenness and exquisitely serves as a cautionary tale to us all (2 Samuel 6:16). Michal foolishly rebuked her husband, King David, because she felt she could stand in judgment of King David's choice of praise toward God. It is not my contention, and I cannot stress this point too much: emotions are useful, healthy, and necessary.

So, again, we need to emphasize the correct response is not a dead, cold orthodoxy. No, heaven forbid such a loathsome thought. We need to incorporate a finely tuned balance. We must allow for the free expression of human emotions to manifest as the Holy Spirit leads the individual while not tipping the scales too far that we fall prey to the wiles of the devil. Satan is the only victor when Evangelicals attend worship with only emotional stimulation. If the worship experience is genuinely to be holistic, then all three components of the human psyche must be stimulated appropriately: intellect and emotions properly united will guide the Evangelicals to the corresponding volitional actions.

It is my contention what is the far too often experience of the many African American Evangelicals is they leave the Sunday worship with only a weak, anemic emotional encounter. I cannot even posit they do experience an encounter with God Himself as He only enters the fellowship with those who are worshipping Him in Spirit and Truth (John 4).

WEIGHED AND FOUND WANTING DUE TO PAROCHIALISM

> He that loveth father or mother more than
> me is not worthy of me: and he that loveth son
> or daughter more than me is not worthy of me
> (Matthew 10:37).

My people, right or wrong, my people!

It is most unfortunate whenever people gravitate to the end of an extreme on any continuum. It is usually best to be somewhere in the middle. I grant that approach would not be sexy or garner much attention (which is the big problem in our culture as one only needs to look at the Kardashian phenomenon), but this approach is over the long haul the safest place to want to be when it is all said and done. For instance, it is unhealthy to get *no exercise*. Yet, we all know someone who ventures into the realm of narcissism or, even worse, becomes obsessed with physical beauty, culminating in dangerous health effects (think baseball and their steroid fiasco). I shudder to live in a world absent of any sports whatsoever, but one's love of sports has ruined many marriages and other social constructs. There are always exceptions, of course, but there is much wise counsel to be heeded in rejecting excess in either direction.

Tragically, African American history has been fraught with negativity with anything "attached to blackness" for much of the history in America. While it might be considered a silly or inconsequential example, I nonetheless point out the origin of "Black Friday." Black Friday is the name given to the shopping day after Thanksgiving.

People coined the phrase *Black Friday* because the volume of shoppers created traffic accidents and sometimes even violence. Police coined the phrase to describe the mayhem surrounding the congestion of pedestrian and auto traffic in downtown shopping areas.[41]

I would venture to guess not many non-African American females grew up playing with African American dolls. I believe it is safe to postulate many African American families can easily recount their young females playing with Caucasian dolls as they grew up. I know quite a few of my female relatives and friends certainly grew up playing with Caucasian Barbie and Ken dolls. Yet I believe it would be equally safe to postulate almost to a near certainty no Caucasian young females even gave thought to play with a Negro doll. Society has masterly ingrained the debilitating belief (primarily to people of color) that being "white" was considered virtuous and noble. All one needs to do is view an old western where the good guys dress in what color? White! What colors were the bad guys? You guessed it! Black!

Self-Inflicted Wounds

Many thoughts begin to flood my thoughts even as I contemplate the words to write this chapter. As I ponder this topic, a scene from Spike Lee's epic, *Malcolm X* begins to marinate in my mind. Malcolm Little (later known as Malcolm X) grew up hustling in the streets of Omaha, Nebraska, during the 1940s and, like many of his male Negro (accepted moniker of that time) contemporaries Malcolm endured the painful process of "perming" his hair.[42] Why? Because *nappy hair* was not considered "beautiful" in the larger Caucasian dominated culture of the times. As a result, Negroes came, in large part, to accept this ultimately self-inflicted wound. I pause

---

[41] Amadeo, Kimberly. "Why Black Friday is called Black Friday." *The Balance.* 22 November 2019, https://www.thebalance.com/why-is-it-called-black-friday-3305712.

[42] A perm is a hairstyle consisting of waves or curls set into the hair. The curls may last a number of months, hence the name. I am making specific reference to the African American male participation as many African American females still undertake the practice.

to say I intentionally choose to use the term "self-inflicted" because regardless of external concepts or cultural expectations, the individual, properly understood, should be the final and ultimate arbiter as to what is beautiful to them. Most come to accept the maxim, "beauty is in the eye of the beholder." Yet, historically we have come to understand who controls the story controls how the narrative is packaged, communicated, and eventually received into the culture. Until very recently, the story packaged, communicated, and received was essentially devoid of any enduring African American input or favorable consideration. Thus, what was considered beautiful was the unrealistic and, ironically, totally sexist and misogynistic concept of the ubiquitous doll, *Barbie,* and later her male companion, *Ken* as national symbols of aesthetic beauty.

Sadly, the more I reflect, the more I came to understand how this malaise negatively affected me as an African American male trying to make his way into this sordid world of aesthetics. The stereotype of African Americans' tendency to possess "large lips" plagued me for most of my formative years. Whenever I would pose for a picture, I would purposely *tuck in my lips* in a vain attempt to make them appear smaller. One prominent example is the picture my wife and I posed for on the day of my promotion to Lieutenant Colonel in the US Army. This picture was my *Facebook* profile picture for the longest time as it captured a very significant occasion in my military career. Every time I looked (until very recently) at this picture, I felt plagued with guilt for being ashamed of how my lips made me feel unattractive.

I am delighted to report, by the grace of God, these thoughts of inadequacy no longer dominate me. As a witty aside, my wife would heartily insist I have sifted to that other extreme I warned of at the beginning of this chapter, but that is a discussion for another day. Yet I understand I am able to come to this conclusion at the ripe old age of fifty-five. Still, tragically I spent so much of my past in self-inflicted defeat because of the external perceptions foisted upon African Americans, which far too many of us unwittingly accept hook, line, and sinker to our own demise.

Yet as is often the case, our remedy to one extreme is to unwisely swing the pendulum, not back to the middle, but the other extreme. The 1960s were a volatile time in America. Americans experienced the hippie movement, which embraced an extreme, a seemingly almost *anti-everything* worldview. There was the controversial war in Vietnam that dominated the nightly news and America's collective conscience. The Civil Rights Movement was in full swing, which eventually spawned a movement that would eventually embrace a more militant movement called "Black Power." It seemed the world seem headed to a radical embrace of anarchy. Heroes were such radicals as Angela Davis, Malcolm X, Huey Newton, and Marcus Garvey from the African American community as well as Timothy Leary, Jane Fonda and Gloria Steinem from the more conventional mainstream Caucasian community.

Boy, I was only a youngster, but the sixties were a time where the Negro began to find their voice for the first time in America. *I am Black, and I am Proud* became the new unofficial Negro National Anthem. Marvelously, on so many levels, for the first-time many *People of Color* began to boast with pride in their race. African Americans saw gains in the entertainment world, in the arts, in sports, and every component of life that mattered, even politically. African Americans like Jesse Owens, Hattie McDaniel, Benjamin O. Davis, Joe Louis, Jackie Robinson, and Cassius Clay (who later would come to be known as Muhammad Ali) began to eradicate the perception of the inferiority of the African American.

Serendipitously, history reveals on many levels as with the important virtues of these newfound voices came, as one might expect, the corollary vices of any human enterprise. People, rooted in a proper biblical anthropology, will readily concede all human endeavors become inevitably contaminated with sin. Evangelicals never place any confidence, on any real level, upon the unmitigated ascent of humanity. Yes, Evangelicals happily acknowledge that humanity is capable of great acts of altruism. Still, as the Tower of Babel freely demonstrates, that same humanity is capable of great human debacles as well. Evangelicals understand mixed within this capacity is the inescapable and indelible marks of the Fall. Due to common grace, humanity still retains the image of God, but it is still true all of humanity possesses an image of God marred by the effects of sin. Thus, the African American experience is just like any other human enterprise: a mixture of great feats coupled with great folly.

Thus, two different realities can be true at the same time and in the same relationship. African Americans Evangelicals could then and should still today rejoice in the celebration of our heritage, our culture, and our unique contribution to God's greatest act of creation: humanity! There is nothing inherently evil in rejoicing in the declaration that *I'm Black and I am proud.* There is a profound beauty in the texture of our hair, the fullness of our lips, the unique bodily dimensions of our females, our protruding lips, etc., etc. These features do not signify superiority or inferiority; they still signal the uniqueness of our ethnicity. It does not mean African Americans are better or worse than any other ethnicity. It just demonstrates African Americans are different; we are fully equal and valid parts of God's tapestry that makes being human part of God's masterpiece, with the man being the capstone of His creative acts.

What Makes Me "Me"

The issue becomes when African American Evangelicals take that worldview concerning ethnicity and make it our bellwether identity marker. While I am proud to be an African American, my ethnic identity cedes far into the background as far as what ultimately defines me as a person. I believe the average African American, to include some African American Evangelicals (even unwittingly), allow their ethnicity to become their chief identity marker. While I view myself as *Evangelical African American,* I believe most of my African American brethren seem to adopt an *African American Evangelical* identity. Lest you think this to be a case of meaningless, abstract semantic nitpicking that does not amount to a hill of beans, let me attempt to illustrate why I believe this not to be the case.

I, like everyone else, am a passive recipient in all that is associated with my humanity. I had no input whatsoever in being born male, in being born to James and Ethel Kyles, in inheriting the genes, which greatly impact my skills and ability. I was born with my ethnicity wholly due to the sovereign decree of God. I was born in 1964, not in 1944. I was born in Brooksville, Mississippi, not in Detroit, Michigan. I was born to economically disadvantaged African American parents, not to affluent Caucasian parents. I write as an adult who now better understands all of these factors. These factors and so many others beyond my control that directly impact my identity are part of God's marvelous plan to complete His masterpiece, which ends with God conforming me to the image of His dear Son, Jesus Christ of Nazareth.

While I am immensely proud of how God has uniquely created me as He has, it is still not my African American identity, which shapes me or defines me. What defines me is my union with God's only-begotten Son. My union with Jesus Christ as my personal Lord and Savior is what radically transforms my life. The Holy Writ uses language like, *"Therefore if any man be in Christ, he is a new creation: old things are passed away; behold all things are become new"* (2 Corinthians 5:17), or *"When I was a child, I spake like a child, I understood as a child, I thought as a child: but when I became a man, I put away childish things"* (1 Corinthians 13:11).

I am fully cognizant some will take offense as a reflective self-defense mechanism. They will take exception to the characterization of childishness. They will rebuff me as an *out of touch fundamentalist* who is akin to the cranky old man who is yelling at people to get off his front lawn. Yet many of these same people who will readily attend the worship service at their local place of worship and participate in worship services where it is customary to preface any public discourse with some statement along these lines, "I give honor to God (or Christ) who is the head of my life." My simple query is why is God (or Christ) not the head of their lives when African American Evangelicals enter the ballot booth? This phenomenon is reminiscent of when James wrote in his Epistle the following words, *"For if any be a hearer of the word and not a doer, he is like unto a man beholding his natural face in a glass: For he beholdeth himself, and goeth his way ,and straightway forgetteth what manner of man he was"* (James 1:23–24). I submit for the reader's consideration these arresting words vividly portray the exact offense I am laying at the feet of the African American Evangelical community.

Evangelicals are blithely attending Churches throughout the great landscape of America, praising God and acknowledging Him as the head of our lives, as the fountainhead of all our blessings, Sunday after Sunday, Bible Study after Bible Study, Sunday school after Sunday school, yet when we engage in political affairs, we do so in a manner wholly antithetical to how this same God reveals His heart to be on vital matters such as life, marriage, and gender.

How am I able to make such a statement about the worship experience of many African American Evangelicals? Because I have spent the majority of my formative time in African American Churches. I know firsthand the liturgy of the typical African American Evangelical worship experience. Again, there is much to commend for the African American Evangelical worship, several of which I fondly remember and miss. Yet the question remains how it is compatible with claiming heartfelt fidelity with and to Jesus Christ in our worship yet live politically (the focus of this book) in a manner wholly inconsistent with His teachings, both explicit and implicit. This incongruity is much like the nascent ministry of the Apostle Peter. Peter would make bold declarations but then not be able to *cut the mustard* when the rubber hit the road. Peter's eventual transformation is what buffets my hope that many of my African American brethren can be genuine believers even though they err grievously in their political engagement. Satan desires to sift all of Christ's bride as wheat, but thankfully we have Christ's promise the very gates of Hell will not prevail against the only human institution Jesus Christ has promised divine protection: His Bride of Christ, the Church (Matthew 16:18).

My perplexion is how does one, with any true attempt at biblical fidelity, reconcile the notion that Christ is the *head of their life.* Then attempt to politically align themselves with someone or some political entity that makes possible the slaughter of life within the womb, rejects the biblical definition of marriage, and rejects the sovereign gender binary.[43] It is ironic one of the chief criticisms from secularists is that Evangelicals *chuck their brains* at the door when they choose to believe. They accuse Evangelicals of relying on emotions and rejecting a rational look at the evidence. The secular elites accuse the Evangelical community of wanting "heaven" to be real so we can take this radical *leap into the dark* with the hopes we will be caught by "God" on the other side. Many secularists inaccurately accuse Evangelicals of embracing a naïve notion of the afterlife to give us the courage to endure the toils of our vain and ultimately meaningless and inconsequence human existence. As some of the purported great thinkers of our time understand it, without this emotional crutch, the only logical consequence for humanity is suicide, so they surmise.[44]

The Intoxicating Allure of Barack Obama

Tragically, I believe this is similar to what many of my African American Evangelical brethren are similarly doing, many unwittingly. What I mean, they are *chucking their brains* at the door and only thinking through the lens of their ethnicity. They are allowing their identity as African Americans to determine how they engage politically. Ninety-four percent of my African American Evangelical brethren consciously voted for Barack Obama, and I believe one of their chief reasons, frankly I think for many, the only reason, was his ethnicity. They conscientiously chose to cast their ballot for Barack Obama with the full knowledge he supported abortion. I deem with that one issue alone makes any political candidate untenable for any informed and mature in the faith Evangelical to align themselves with politically.

I believe a great many, to include many I know personally and love dearly, African American Evangelicals have adopted a, my *people, right or wrong, my people* mindset. The reasons why are beyond the

---

[43] In African American worship parlance whenever someone spoke during a worship service that would often begin their public discourse with something along with the lines of "I give an honor to God who is the head of my life…"

[44] All one had to do is read and understand the logic and rhetoric of philosophers like Fredrich Nietzsche.

reach of my intellectual prowess, so I will limit my analysis to how I believe this mindset intersects with the theological implications.

The implications, I am afraid, are far-reaching. Most are temporal, of varying magnitudes. It is undeniable that God grants His creation the freedom to make bad choices. Yet, as with any wise parent God permits the bad choices to allow us to live in the light of these bad choices. Some (the Elect) will be disciplined towards more Christlikeness; others (the Reprobate) will be judged to their utter shame. While the secret things belong to God and one cannot associate, with any degree of theological accuracy, a one-to-one correspondence between two events is undoubtedly not out of the realm of possibility what we are experiencing corporately as a nation and specifically as African Americans are in direct relationship to our stewardship as God's prophetic voice upon the Earth. Only eternity will likely reveal as to whether what America in general and African Americans, in particular, are experiencing is in direct response to our lack of adherence to a proper Christian ethic regarding our political engagement. I believe many in the Evangelicals community falsely believe there is no eternal consequential or temporal effect on how we engage in the political arena. As if this is an activity that God takes a *hands-off* approach and lets us play in our sandbox as we see fit.

I believe there is much to be concerned about when we harvest a sense of ethnic pride when that sense of pride collides with our identity with Christ; then, we are no longer walking in solidarity with the tenets of the faith. When we vote for political candidates who affirm what the Bible forbids, then we are not responding as Jesus, nor any of His Apostles would have responded. Can any African American Evangelical honestly attempt to postulate Jesus Christ would support a political position that legitimizes the murder of a person created in His very image? What would be the basis of such a postulation? That the person in the womb is not a human being? I would submit that argument is destroyed with the record of the prophet Jeremiah's birth. When did Jeremiah become a "person," and more importantly, who determines the answer to such an inquiry? Undoubtedly, the Evangelical would heartily affirm that person is none other than God Himself, right? Well, God does not speak with a forked tongue in this matter. He states emphatically, *"**Before** I formed thee in the belly I **knew thee;** before **thou** camest forth out of the womb I sanctified thee, and I ordained thee a prophet unto the nations"* (emphasis mine) (Jeremiah 1:5). Would anyone want to argue this event does not apply to *every* human birth? Is there anyone who wants to dispute the proposition that in the mind of God (the only mind that counts, remember I direct my thesis to my fellow Evangelicals) even before God forms the infant in the womb that God regards that entity as a *Person, deserving of the all the inalienable rights of Personhood enumerated in our venerated Constitution?*

How do we proclaim in our place of worship that Jesus Christ is the *head of our lives* Sunday after Sunday and then make calculated decisions to support political candidates simply because they share our same skin color? I know many will institutively and passionately chaff at such a characterization, but I fail to understand the matter in any other fashion. African American Evangelicals voted for Barack Obama in direct opposition to what they purport to believe and embrace as proper biblical theology. We have spent the better part of our time in America lamenting about how Caucasians act in a manner inconsistent with their cherished Christian heritage. Yet when the first opportunity presented itself, African American Evangelicals committed the same action we have correctly criticized our Caucasian countrymen for in the past.

The only result is in both cases; the name of Christ is sullied, and Evangelicals of both sides of the aisle subject themselves to His hand of discipline. On the one hand, it just affirms what biblically literate Evangelicals already understand. Adam, our first father, marred the entire human race by his disobedience in the garden. On the other hand, it exposes African American Evangelicals as crass hypocrites. When the first opportunity to demonstrate how the people of God can courageously live with fidelity in the face of admittedly difficult choices, 94 percent of the American African Evangelical community still chose *not* to take the narrow road. Instead of seizing the moment and striking a blow for the cause of Christ in overwhelming measure African American Evangelicals demonstrated the same type of parochialism African American Evangelicals have complained our

Caucasian Evangelical brethren for displaying. African American Evangelicals had a chance to be great; I believe we squandered our moment to shine for Christ because we became blind at the allure of getting *one of ours* in the White House.

Getting *one of ours* in the White House or any other place of notoriety is not worth it in the final analysis if it leads to the slaughter of life in the womb, especially when it is African American life that has an outsized part in the massacre.[45] It can never be worth it when God's design for human flourishing through the institution of holy matrimony is abased. It will never be worth it when we can, without blushing, thumb our noses at God and reject His ability to create male and female as He sovereignly wills.

I mentioned at the beginning of this book that I understood as an African American I have the benefits of saying things that a fellow Caucasian Evangelical would not necessarily feel comfortable or believe they are free to express in public conversation. Let there be no mistake; these conversations are still taking place when we get in our personal circles. I do it, and I know you do it as well. There is nothing inherently wrong with such an admission because context and the proper setting are always wise counsel for different types of speech. Yet even I am aware that there are limitations to that freedom for even me as an African American.

Sacred Cows and Hobby Horses

First, let me begin with a bit of levity to set the stage for dealing with a sensitive subject, hopefully. There is a closing scene from the movie *Barbershop II* played by Cedric the Entertainer. Cedric Kyles (no relation as far as I know) played the character Eddie, and Eddie was the barbershop's elder statesman. The storyline of the movie portrayed Eddie as the shop's *wise sage*. As part of the movie background,

---

[45] In 2014, 36% of all abortions were performed on black women, who are just 13% of the female population. Wall Street Journal published an article by Jason Riley where the sub line of the article was, "In New York City, thousands more black babies are aborted each year than born alive. For more information, see www.wsj.com/amp/articles/lets-talk-about-the-black-abortion-rate-1531263697.

Eddie worked alongside the main character, Calvin Palmer's (played by the actor O'Shea Jackson, better known by the professional name *Ice Cube*) father, who was the original shop owner. Eddie was the figure who would speak his mind and say the type of things older people who are outspoken (every family has them) are prone to say. In classic Eddie form, Eddie cannot refrain himself from speaking his mind on things he believes are incorrectly perceived by others. Eddie proceeds to voice his bewilderment over all the hoopla society has placed on Rosa Parks as a national hero. Of course, the regulars who assemble at the barbershop go berserk that Eddie would dare insult the memory of a national treasure in not only African American culture but American culture.

It is not my intention to insult the memory of a national treasure in not only African American culture but American culture. I have wrestled with exactly how I should address the following subject. Do I even include it in the book? How far do I go if I do bring it up? In fact, I discussed the topic with one of my close friends who published his own book just last year. He confirmed what I knew all along. The proper thing to do was address the *elephant in the room* solely in my mind. I realize I must discuss the matter, but know I do so with the highest amount of respect and admiration for all that was accomplished by this person.[46]

Dr. Martin Luther King, Jr. is easily one of the most significant individuals in human history. Nobel Peace prize winner, iconic Civil

---

[46] I was like practically every other African American youth growing up in the seventies and eighties. I idolized Martin Luther King and for good reasons. He achieved and sacrificed so much for the advancement of Colored People. It was a badge of honor for people of the older generation to be able to say, "They marched with King." I am a member of the same fraternity, Alpha Phi Alpha Fraternity Inc., that Dr. King pledged, a fraternity still near and dear to my heart today, and it is not easy to critique a beloved brother in a public discourse such as this. But theology trumps all, and I must love Christ above all else. If I must fall out with anyone, I will always choose the other rather than falling out with my Lord and Savior, Jesus Christ of Nazareth. To any degree, I am out of bounds; I cry out to God, "Have mercy on my soul, a wretched sinner." So, for me, this issue is my elephant in the room. How do I discuss African American parochialism and not discuss the quintessential theological example?

Right worker, one of history's greatest orators, are just a few of the tributes that one can easily recite about the accomplishments of Dr. King's life. Yet despite my appreciation for many of the gains, I benefit greatly and will forever be indebted from Dr. King's service and sacrifice, I nonetheless believe I must acknowledge I find his theological philosophy problematic in the most charitable accounting.

Criticisms across ethnic lines are dicey even when we are the most charitable, and, in most cases, wise counsel would be to avoid engagement whenever possible. It is the same in many other situations. It is always the best course of action if children are in the midst of a group setting for the parent of the child needing correction to address the matter rather than another parent. I do not feel comfortable at all, addressing a female student's failure to adhere to the school's dress code. I believe that should be the purview of other females, especially when the matter addresses particular parts of the female anatomy.

I understand how one might rightly ponder why I would choose to single out such a legendary icon in the African American community for criticism. Some might even interject that is the problem with most Evangelicals in general. The critics say Evangelicals spend way too much time tearing things down and even other people down (even other Evangelicals) than they do building things or people up. It is similar to Mahatma Gandi's famous retort, "I like your Christ, I do not like your Christians. Your Christians are so unlike your Christ."[47] Thus, the skepticism to the wisdom of venturing down this road is duly noted, but I feel duty-bound to address the matter squarely and directly.

The African American community has a long history of looking to the clergy for spiritual leadership and direction. Even during

---

[47] As with many quotes, there is considerable controversy, about whether the person commonly associated with the quote is the actual author. Stanley Jones, a missionary, reports in a book *The Knights Templar & the Protestant Reformation* when he met Mahatma Gandhi, he asked him, "Mr. Gandhi, though you quote the words of Christ often, why is that you appear to so adamantly reject becoming his follower?" Gandhi replied, "Oh, I don't reject Christ. I love Christ. It's just so many of you Christians are so unlike Christ.

slavery, when most African Americans could not read and write, the few who did, I would submit by the providence hand of God, were usually, those who rose to prominence as the community preachers. The African American community has always looked to the clergy as people worthy of grand respect. This level of well-deserved honor gives the clergy a platform that provides them an outsized amount of influence, and power.

While many people clamor for power it is interesting when you hear the testimony of those who rise to the level of significant influence in society. I think of the Supreme Commander of the Allied Expeditionary Forces in Europe, General Dwight E. Eisenhower. General Eisenhower recounts the internal anguish he wrestled with concerning the Allied plan to defeat the German by invading France. While the Allies forces understood the invasion would significantly increase the likelihood of winning World War II; it would be won only at the expense of a significant number of Allied troops.

General Eisenhower came to understand with power also comes even greater responsibility. We can add President Truman and his highly controversial decision to drop the atomic bomb on Japan, which effectively brought an end to the Pacific front of World War II. We have a more contemporary example with former President Barack Obama. President Obama openly shares the personal angst he felt when he authorized American Special Forces to execute a mission to capture Osama Bin Laden.

The Bible weighs in the matter when it says, *"for unto whomsoever much is given, of him shall much be required"* (Luke 12:48). The brother of Jesus Christ, James, warns in his Epistle, *"My brethren, be not many masters, knowing that we shall receive the greatest condemnation."* (James 3:1). So, it is the Bible that informs my decision to address the legacy of Dr. King on the African American Evangelical community.

I believe the central problem in African American Evangelical theology is the failure to diagnose the problem accurately. The fundamental problem in the African American community is not *white privilege*; it is not *racism*; it is not *economic suppression* or even *voter disenfranchisement*. It is not because African Americans have never

111

received their *forty acres and a mule*. I do not dispute these (as well as many, many others) are grave matters and ones that due consideration and attention are duly warranted. As one contemporary example, racism is real, and it remains a toxic blight on humanity. Good-willed men and women everywhere should expend all energies and resources at their disposal to combat this stain on God's good creation.

Yet, any social ill you could conceivably enumerate will never rise to the level of the root cause. The root cause of *all societal ills* is *man's old thorn in the side* in the human experience: SIN. The issue of *sin* takes us back to the theological necessity of understanding the *bad news* if one indeed comes to appreciate the *good news*, i.e., The Gospel. My chief criticism of Dr. King, in particular, and others like Jesse Jackson and Al Sharpton, in general, is their message does not *explicitly* present the *Gospel* as *the* answer.

I would submit a legitimate case can be made to charge these individuals with ministerial malpractice. Most people readily recognize each of these individuals (and I could list others) with the moniker *Reverend*. It is the Reverend Dr. Martin Luther King Jr. It is the Reverend Jesse Jackson. It is the Reverend Al Sharpton. Yet, what are each of these individuals known to offer as solutions to the societal ills for the people they purport to speak for and represent?

The Gospel is curiously and consistently always missing in their response. I challenge anyone to recount a clear, unambiguously presentation of the Gospel from Dr. King as he spoke, and there is a tremendous inventory of his public statements we have at our disposal to dissect. Using the *I Have a Dream* speech from the *March on Washington* in 1963 as one example, can anyone point to any statement made that day that a Muslim Imam or a Jewish Rabbi could not equally proclaim?

Can anyone point to an explicitly frank and direct presentation of the Gospel as the remedy for African American oppression at any point during King's time as the prominent African American clergy voice during the Civil Rights Movement? Voter registration is essential; equal access to housing and education are important issues. Again, the list could go on and on, but the crucial dilemma will always remain. Answer the wrong problem, and you will invariably arrive at the wrong solution.

God does not commission or call Evangelical ministers to solve temporal issues, at least not as their primary mission. God did not send His only begotten Son into the world to address slavery, and slavery was prevalent during the times of Christ. God, the Father, did not send Christ to fight for women's liberation, and women faced severe marginalization during the ministry of Christ. The First Person of the Trinity did not send the second Person of the Trinity into *time and space* to solve the economic disparity. However, there was rampant economic despair present while Christ walked the Earth.

Dr. King was guilty of preaching and addressing what some scholars have coined as *The Social Gospel*.[48] Yet the Social Gospel is not the calling of the Gospel minister, so I circle back to James's warning: not many of us should become teachers for teachers will be held to the strictest standards. It is, for this reason, I lay blame at the feet of Rev. Dr. Martin Luther King. He had a tremendous platform, but I regrettably believe the theological record will find him weighed and found wanting.

I did not envy the sensitive waters that Pastor John Piper had to navigate when he spoke at the MLK 50 Ceremony. *The Gospel Coalition, a highly respected Evangelical Group*, hosted this historic

---

[48] The Social Gospel seeks to apply Christian ethics to social problems such as poverty, slums, poor nutrition and education, alcoholism, crime, and war. The critics of the Social Gospel movement believe temporal concerns are emphasized while the doctrines of sin, salvation, heaven, and hell, and the future kingdom of God were downplayed. I believe the Social Gospel is not a legitimate activity Evangelicals are to participate in to accomplish the Great Commission. Jesus never issued any call for political change, not even by peaceful means. Jesus Christ did not understand His mission was to come to earth to be a political or social reformer. The Gospel Jesus preached never sought to address social reform, or social justice or political change. Jesus understood what was necessary to bring reconciliation between God and fallen man was not reforming man-made institutions like the government, which are made up of depraved human beings, but it would be accomplished by changing hearts and minds. Christ, like the Apostles that followed Him, preached the saving power of the Gospel and the sanctifying work of the Holy Spirit.

event in 2018. While there can be no dispute regarding the prominent and vital role Dr. King played in the struggles for Civil Rights for all people but especially for African Americans, I believe the legitimate and fair question is, "was it a Christ-centric affair?"

I appreciate Dr. Piper's ginger treatment of Dr. King's theological record. It is surely an undoubtedly, delicate tightrope how far one can go when you speak at a ceremony ostensibly celebrating the life of the honoree? Listening to a Todd Friel podcast (where I acquired my information about Dr. Piper's comments), Friel made the following insightful observation:

> Theology is more important than racial issues. If that was offensive to you, hold on. Theology is more important than abortion; theology is more important than sexual issues. Theology is more important than any issue because it is a representation of God's character in nature.[49]

This is what Dr. Piper, who was the only person with the courage to speak frankly about commonly known knowledge regarding King's theological positions said during the ceremony.[50]

> He [King] was blinded to the beauty and truth as Christ's majesty as Creator of the

---

[49] Todd Friel made these comments during his podcast, *Wretched Radio*, dated April 9, 2018. https://www.youtube.com/watch?v=AvmimB8hNrA

[50] Prominent Evangelicals who attended and/or participated in the MLK 50 include Matt Chandler, H. B. Charles, Don Carlson, Beth Moore, Russell Moore and Thabiti Anyabwile. The issue, for me, is not whether it was proper to attend or not; the issue, for me, becomes what message do we convey by our public pronouncement as part of the event. I believe only Dr. Piper struck the right chord. We can certainty laud a person for their contributions without skimming the facts or not addressing the elephant in the room. If one would reach the conclusion that the ceremony was the improper venue to address the "elephant in the room" then other decisions would need to be considered as to the advisability of attending said events.

Universe, blinded to the glory of Christ's grace
in suffering imputed guilt from others, blinded
to the all-encompassing authority of Christ that
he received when he rose bodily from the dead.

Ladies and gentlemen, this is not some rebuke of a doctrinal
issue like the debate about the age of the Earth or the validity of certain instruments during the worship service or even something more
important to Evangelical life like the proper mode of baptism. No,
my friends, this issue cuts right across the fabric of the Gospel itself.
It is not enough to postulate Christ rose from the grave. Evangelicals
are keen on insisting upon the explicit adherence to a belief in the
bodily resurrection of Jesus Christ. King apparently was only willing
to grant that Christ rose spiritually. Theology is not like horseshoes;
when it comes to first-order doctrinal topics, getting close is not
good enough.

The question before us is whether the views of Friel, Pipers and
those who toe this party line is consistent with the mind of God. If
so, to be celebrated and emulated or is this much ado about nothing
and people should mind their business, especially when it comes to
the religious philosophy of others. One of the jokes in the Southern
Baptist Convention (SBC) life is the Eleventh Commandment is
Thy Shall not Criticize a Fellow Southern Baptist. Well, the last three
churches I have been a member of have been SBC churches, and I
guess I never got or signed the memo because I do not subscribe to
such expression.

I think it adds important insight to add what Piper went on to
say during his remarks at the MLK 50 celebration, "In his early 20's
Martin Luther King turned away from these great objective biblical realities, and you can read about it with sadness in many of his
papers in those days," Piper added. I don't know if he came home.
Many believe he did. [A speaker], in the [earlier] panel, documented
to the point at which he thought he came home...and met God in a
profound way. I hope so." I join with Piper and hope that Dr. King
did come home, but to the best of my research and understanding,
I cannot find any clear and unambiguous renunciation of Dr. King's

earlier held erroneous beliefs. I believe it is fair his beliefs can be most charitably be classified as troublesome and at worst case as heretical.[51]

So while I will not attempt to display the hubris of Eddie, I will still, nonetheless, draw our attention to the ministry of Dr. Martin Luther King Jr. as another vivid example of African American Evangelicals' embrace and cherishment to what is antithetical to orthodox Evangelicalism. I would be quick to include other purported figures like Jesse Jackson and Al Sharpton in this category. For sake of brevity, I will not elaborate on Jackson and Sharpton other than to say they are guilty of the same theological malfeasance of King and so many others who carry religious, Evangelical titles but do not espouse or communicate principles consistent with Evangelical orthodoxy or orthopraxy. The same issues I raise concerning the ministry of Dr. King, I lay at the feet of African Americans figures like Jackson and Sharpton, especially those of the clergy.

I do so soberly and with great fear and trembling, but I do so because I believe the African American Evangelical community is experiencing grave and irreparable harm. There are innumerable other influential African American names I could add to this list, yet when one attempts to enter a strong man's house and plunder his goods, they must first bind the strong man (Mark 3:27). So if we are going to address the African American Evangelical drift from orthodox Evangelicalism, we have to include the ministry of Dr. Martin Luther King.

No one is above approach. The Apostle Paul proved that when he confronted the Apostle Peter to his face when he was displaying inconsistency (Galatians 2:11–21). Again, Peter found himself on the end of Christ's sharp rebuke when Peter attempted to dissuade

---

[51] Coretta Scott King, widow of Dr. King, in 1996 flew to San Francisco to ask Stanford Professor Clayborne Carson to examine and provide his theological analysis of writings found from Dr. King. The collection includes documents from 1948 to 1963 and Carson believes they "get us closer to King's true identity" because they shed new light on how he [King] viewed the Bible, Carson said. The writings reveal King didn't believe the story of Jonah being swallowed by a whale was true or that John the Baptist actually met Jesus. King once referred to the Bible as "mythological" and also doubted whether Jesus was born to a virgin, Carson said. See www.sfgate.com/news/article/Writings-show-King-as-liberal-Christian-2623685.

Christ from going the way of the Cross (Mark 8:33). Although many professing believers in the Evangelical *claim* they do not hold *sacred cows* I find that not to be the case when certain buttons are pressed.

As two quick recent examples, I had some unpleasant experiences that may be beyond repair (hey, I am keeping it *one hundred* as the young folks are fond of saying). The most recent example was my publicly stated opposition to the ministry of the aforementioned Beth Moore. Even after providing irrefutable documentation from respected theologians like Phil Johnson of *Grace to You* ministries and noted apologist Justin Peters detailing Moore's excursion into highly dubious beliefs and actions, I ran into severe opposition and rebuke. Mind you, when I asked for an intellectual argument to illustrate where I was off-base, I received: *nada, zilch!* The only response I received was, "I like her, and she is a great Bible teacher." I hope the reader can see that response for what it is: a person with a sacred cow, a person who says, "Don't confuse me with the facts." A person making an emotive defense as opposed to a rational intellectual defense.

The other occasion was my rebuke of Republicans for their political chancery of then-President Obama's Supreme Court nominee, Merrick Garland. The Republicans, led by Senate Majority Leader Mitch McConnell, refused to bring Garland's nomination before the US Senate for confirmation. The Democrats attempted the same technique when President Trump nominated Brett Kavanaugh to fill the latest Supreme Court opening. I had the gall to posit in public conversation how hypocritical it was for Republicans to cry foul when they were in the same situation they did the same exact thing. A member of my Church felt I was criticizing the candidacy of Brett Kavanaugh and proceeded to blast me on social media for not supporting a "Brother in Christ."

Outside of two crucial facts, I have no problems with my opponent's strong rebuke.

1. I was making no critique whatsoever on the merits or demerits of Kavanaugh's candidacy (I actually supported his candidacy).

2. I do not regard Brett Kavanaugh as my "Brother in Christ" as no properly informed Evangelical would as well. There is a reason Evangelicals are understood to be part of the branch of Christianity termed as Protestantism. My Lord, the root part of the word is *protest*. It is both frightening and appalling the average Evangelical demonstrates no awareness there is a profound theological difference between Evangelicalism and Roman Catholicism. Vatican II *still* places an *anathema* upon anyone who espouses salvation is by faith and *faith alone*.[52] I will save some readers the trouble. An *anathema* is placing a curse upon someone to be eternally damned.[53] It is the very language the Apostle Paul used in Galatians 1:8–9 when he wrote, *"But though we, or an angel from heaven, preach any other gospel unto you than which we have preached unto you, let him be accursed [anathema]. As we said before, so say I now again, If any man preach any other gospel unto you than that ye have received, let them be accursed [anathema]."* Let there be no mistake what the Apostle Paul is saying. He is saying he (with the full power and authority of heaven behind him) places a divine curse of eternal damnation upon anyone who dares to preach a different Gospel than the Gospel that he was preaching. It is in that same exact vein that Rome is placing upon Evangelicals for their embrace of the doctrine that salvation is wholly and exclusively by faith alone. My friend, the person embracing Roman Catholicism is not my Brother in Christ. Thus, I have no problem whatsoever affirming the judicial qualifications of Brett Kavanaugh, but sorry, our political affinity does not make him one of

---

[52] Vatican II (1962–1965) was the twenty-first ecumenical council of the Roman Catholic Church, announced by Pope John XXIII as a means of spiritual renewal for the church and as an occasion for Christians separated from Rome to join in a search for Christian unity.

[53] Anathema specifically say, "If anyone says that by faith alone the impious are justified (that nothing else is required to obtain justification and that it is not necessary to use one's own will), let him be anathema."

us [Evangelical]. You see, doctrine is always lurking in the background.

We cannot afford to play favorites when it comes to theology. Truth is truth, and falsehoods are falsehoods. It matters not to me in the slightest if the person is African American, a member of my fraternity, an American or a German, a man or a woman. Theology trumps all, and all fall subordinate to God and His revelation. Everyone and everything must bow the knee. God is the only absolute source of truth. He alone reveals what is true and proper and fitting for all of His creations, especially for Evangelicals.

Thus, I must make the conclusion on all the data available to me that Dr. King is weighed and found wanting. I hold out hope like Piper and so many others that Dr. King, did in fact, *come home.* I have purposely made no reference to any of the well documented moral foibles of Dr. King as I am wise enough to understand no one living in a glass house should throw stones. (Ephesians 6:10–18) The ground at the foot of Christ is level and with any assembly of sinners I would be first in line as the chief of sinners. Yet, with all of that being 100 percent true, Evangelicals retain no heretical beliefs. That is why I chose the identity marker *Evangelical.* Evangelicals maintain the belief that the essence of the Gospel consists of the doctrine of salvation by grace alone, solely through faith in Christ's atonement. We believe in the centrality of the conversion or "born-again" experience in receiving salvation, in the authority of the Bible as God's revelation, and in the spreading of the Christian message. Now, much, much more can be added, but there cannot be less.

African American Evangelicals, it is not principally the job of the *John Pipers* of the Evangelical community to call us to repentance, that principal job belongs to you and me. We are the very ones who should be able to appreciate and cherish the secular achievements of men like Dr. King yet honestly address and recognize when beliefs and actions fall beyond the pale. I believe Piper strikes the exact right cord when he said of God's use of King, "I am thankful to God that He made Martin Luther King the human instrument in the renovation of that [segregated] world."

I join Piper in thanking God, the same God who used King Cyprus to send the Israelites back to Jerusalem. The same God who used King Nebuchadnezzar to illustrate God's sovereignty to Shadrach, Meshach, and Abednego (Daniel 3). Yet two disparate things can be true at the same time. God can mightily use a human figure, and that same human figure can still be pagan and a person whose theology should not be emulated by an Evangelical seeking to posit fidelity to Jesus Christ and the Gospel.

As much as I can appreciate the historical significance of Barack Obama and Martin Luther King in world history, African American Evangelicals still have no choice but to place them *outside the ark* based on their stated theological beliefs and practices.[54] Hopefully, we do so with tears, heartache, and pain, holding out hope they *come home* before they take their last breath. We can speak in the present tense concerning Barack Obama and we can only hope at a time in the past with Dr. King.

This was not an easy chapter to write, but it was a chapter I felt I must address. I have attempted to be as accurate as possible in any estimation. I want to again acknowledge my admiration and appreciation for the dignity associated with all that Dr. King and President Obama was able to accomplish. Dr. King, for his oratory excellence, and his financial sacrifice, his familial sacrifice, and ultimately his willingness of personal sacrifice. President Obama for the class and sense of reverence and elegance he and Michelle Obama brought to the Oval Office. Like my seminary president, Dr. Albert Mohler, I do not have to *demonize* the person I come to disagree with theologically or politically. God created both of these gentlemen in His very

---

[54] I want to draw a sharp distinction when I refer to practices. When I speak of practices, I do not have in mind personal sins. I am speaking of individual beliefs that lead to actions by the person and/or those who align themselves with the person's stated belief. Barack Obama personally states he is personally against abortion, yet he oversaw an administration that legitimatized and gave express license to the slaughter of life in the womb. When it was within his power to fight with all of his might the overturning of Roe v. Wade, he worked to broaden not mitigate the practice of abortion, i.e., his embrace of partial-birth abortions.

own image and thus, regardless of our differences, are lives worthy of dignity and respect and admiration when dignity, respect, and admiration are warranted.

CONCLUSION AND PROPOSED SOLUTIONS

It is getting late in the evening, and the sun is going
   down
Get right church and let's go home
Get right church and let's go home
I'm going home on the midnight train

I must work the works of Him that sent me, while
   it is day; the night cometh, when no man can
   work (John 9:4)

During my military career, I was fortunate to learn so many principles that have served me well not only for a successful military career
but helped shape my overall leadership philosophy, my ability to
apply critical thinking, and the need to always bring concentrated
solutions to issues. I must admit I had to learn the last attribute, the
old-fashioned hard way. I was a junior major on my first assignment
as a full-time Officer in the US Army. The US Army assigned me
to the Eighty-Fifth Training Division in Arlington Heights, Illinois,
a suburb of Chicago. Chicago is a typical Midwestern city, which
means the summer can be pretty hot and muggy. Unfortunately, the
work location the Army assigned me; the building had problems
with the air conditioning so frequently it was pretty uncomfortable,
especially if the portable AC units went down, which was often the
case. After weeks of frustration with no apparent end in sight, I had
the bright idea to send an email registering my complaint to my

Brigade Commander. Now, I need to provide a little more context to set the stage properly.

I was a full-time soldier in a US Army Reserves unit. That meant I was one of three full-time service members in the entire unit. Everyone else, to include my Brigade Commander, were reservists, which meant they only came to work (drill as we call it) one weekend a month. Since the reservists only came to work one weekend a month, they did not usually experience any problems (it always seemed steps were taken to ensure things were operational for drill weekends). Since the issue primarily only negatively impacted me and the other two full-time servicemembers, there did not seem to be a lot of energy and effort to provide a permanent remedy. So in a moment of frustration, I fired off the aforementioned, carefully crafted email to my boss. What seemed like a prudent decision on my part at the time turned out to be a colossal faux pas on my part. Instead of receiving a reply *thanking me* for making my boss aware of the deplorable work conditions I was experiencing and assuring me things would change immediately I received a severe (and now understandable) rebuke.

I learned a precious lesson that day. The lesson I learned (the hard way) and earnestly took to heart is you don't bring problems to your boss without having proposed solutions from which the leaders have an option to choose.[55] Leaders in business, and people, in general, do not appreciate having additional problems added to their already taxing environment.

People have enough on their plates with the normal day-to-day grind of life, so this book would not be well-served if it just pointed out what I believed are the issues in the African American Evangelical community concerning their political engagement and fail to offer my proposed solutions to remedy the situation. We should all thank God, He does more than just provide the *Law*. Evangelicals rightfully and gloriously praise His holy name because God provides *Grace*. If

---

[55] It is an important caveat; the superior may choose an entirely different option that the subordinate presents as a proposed solution. Still, the general rule for subordinates raising an issue is to think through situations, so the leader can stay focused on the *big picture* and not get bogged down in the minutiae.

there was no "Good News" available to mankind, then there is no need for much of a Bible after the Fall.

Granted, we may arrive at heaven, and God will reveal my proposed solutions were not the best course of action, or maybe my proposals would be tweaked or modified in some manner to remedy the issue, and that would still be considered a win-win for all parties involved. I will certainly not have the last word or necessarily the best word. It was never God's design that any one person would carry the whole freight. Evangelicals should understand this principle better than most. No one Evangelical possesses all of the gifts administered by the Holy Spirit. We need the entire body using their gifts and callings to function at optimal efficiency. I could be part of the team, decreed by God before time began, to plant the seed; others could be selected to come afterward and water the seed. Yet God, and God alone, has the final word as to whether there will be any increase, and if there is (*Praise the Lord*); any increase, God unilaterally determines the extent of the increase.

A wise exegete will have to admit there are times they have to concede they are not absolutely sure what a given text is saying, yet they are pretty sure what that text *is not* saying.[56] For instance, I do not have the foggiest what precisely the Apostle Paul really meant when he spoke about members of the Corinthian Church being baptized on behalf of the dead in 1 Corinthians 15:29. Yet, I am still pretty confident he did not intend for me to practice this ritual on behalf of my deceased love ones.

So while I do not profess with *absolute certitude* to have the answer to the problem of exactly how African American Evangelical are to engage politically, I would submit with *absolute certitude* there is a major problem in the African American Evangelical community as it pertains to their current political engagement. I remained convinced there is no way 94 percent of *any theological entity* could live with proper orthodoxy and proper orthopraxy and be politically

---

[56] An exegete is a person who uses established principles to draw out of the message of the message the author intended and the original audience would have understood.

aligned with the Democratic Party, as presently constituted, and there be rejoicing in heaven. I am still awaiting someone to make a cogent argument how about it is either possible I am incorrect about heaven not rejoicing or why it is proper for African American Evangelicals to rejoice in their political alignment with the Democratic Party.

As grievous and bleak the current political disposition is in the African American Evangelical Church, thankfully the situation is not under the curse of the unpardonable sin. There is still time to remedy the situation.[57] Using the metaphor of day and night; it is still "daytime." Yet, we do not know how long the light will remain lit. Yes, one of the glorious attributes of God is His long-suffering, His patience, but even with God, there is an expiration date on Grace and Mercy. Thus, there remains a need for a sense of urgency, both individually and corporately, in the African American Evangelical community.

First, let me deal with the matter from an individual perspective. As much as I keep referring to 94 percent of the African American Evangelical community, this is still the matter of individual accountability. Let us never forget, one day, every one of us, we will stand before God *mano-a-mano*. All feeble attempts at justification; God will summarily dismiss, and that is even if there are opportunities to muster a defense. I tend not to believe individuals get much of a chance, if any at all, of a chance to plead our case in the presence of the God of all God, King of all Kings, Lord of all Lords! There is a passage in the Book of Romans where Paul speaks of God shutting every mouth, and the whole world is held accountable (Romans

---

[57] Time is a fluid concept. We plan for the future even though we are fully aware we are not guaranteed to be part of the future. Evangelicals either die, without warning, before the return of Jesus Christ or Christ returns at the Rapture, yet we are good stewards; we still plan. Thus, I am not making a reckless statement, not appreciating the need for urgency. The road to hell will be paved with people with good intentions. There is a popular story of two young girls who went to church with the intent to come forward to be saved. One girl changed her mind at the last minute. She then proceeded to say she would do it next week, but unfortunately, she died before the next week came. The moral of the story is do not wait before it is too late. Unfortunately, there will be countless people who waited too long, and like the unwise virgins were not ready when the bridegroom arrived.

3:19). I would expect our encounter on Judgment Day to be more of a monologue than a dialogue, for sure.

It is astonishing when society assigns blame; it usually is externally focused rather than internally focused. When a couple is experiencing marital issues, each spouse usually focuses primarily, if not, exclusively on the foibles of their significant other. It is the same in many different dimensions: Democrats place all of the blame for the country's ill on obstinate Republicans. The President communicates to the American people that Congress is to blame for stagnation and gridlock in Washington. Congress in-kind replies the blame lays at the feet of whatever President is in office though generally most vociferously from the opposing party. Young people blame their parent's generation for perpetuating greed and social malfeasance into the culture. In contrast, the older generation is apoplectic about the direction young people want to take the country.

What is missing from all of these situations, as well as countless others, is a lack of self-accountability. I admit it took me several years into my marriage to come to the realization the greatest weakness in my marriage was none other than yours truly. I assure you this is not an attempt at false piety; it is both objectively and subjectively true in all of its dimensions. While I can easily point to issues my wife *may* be guilty of since I never can really penetrate into the inner recesses of her soul, I can (and frankly often do) easily assign false blame or motive to many of her actions when conflict arises. Of course, when in doubt, conversely, I always give *myself* the benefit of the doubt. Isn't it funny how often we tend to usually cast *ourselves* in the *most favorable light* but yet cast the other person in the most unflattering light possible? Our *go-to move,* in most cases, is to ascribe the worst possible motive to others. This one truth really illustrates the concept of human depravity so much so we can readily understand the concept if no other example was present in the human experience.

Every year the school where I teach, like most other schools, holds a convocation to begin the school year. A convocation is where all the school personnel, to include cafeteria workers, custodians, bus drivers and many other support staff, assemble at a centrally located place to hear from key district personnel so we may rally together to set the tone for an anticipated awesome, educationally productive school year. Each school usually has school-specific t-shirts designed to create an atmosphere of *es spirit de corps*. The typical highlight of the convocation is with an address from the Superintendent and the event culminates with a featured speaker who *gains notoriety* for some innovation or achievement of scholastic excellence.

One recent speaker sticks out prominently in my mind. He spoke of how the culture in Education in America has changed so radically in just a few short years. He showed a cartoon to dramatically illustrate his point. The cartoon depicted a young student (the young man in the comic could not have been more than ten years old) not meeting academic standards. On the left side of the cartoon, there is "Little Johnny" looking sheepishly down as *his parents and his teacher* look *disapprovingly down at* Little Johnny, clearly communicating, "*We* know *you* can have done a whole lot better, Johnny, and *we* are extremely disappointed in *you*. *You* have to do better!" On the other side of the comic, you had Johnny *with* his parents collectively looking *disapprovingly at* Johnny's teacher, clearly communicating, "*We* know *you* can have done a whole lot better teaching Johnny, and *we* are incredibly disappointed in you. Totally typical of how we process blame today in the culture. It is no wonder we are in the pickle we are currently experiencing.

The Apostle Peter revealed that judgment would begin first with the family of God (1 Peter 4:17). I believe Evangelicals will do well to recapture the mindset that judgment will begin first with us as individuals. Concerning my role as husband, as one example, it serves me no good to fixate on what God will say to my spouse, Monique, about her role as wife and mother as He assesses our marriage. I would do well to *only* concentrate on what God will *say to me* about my role as husband and father as He provides His assessment of our marriage. I tell you it was that one realization, alone, that has saved my marriage and my overall sanity. Now, don't get me wrong, there are still the issues associated with my marriage as there will always be with any human enterprise, but this realization has allowed me to successfully navigate the choppy waters of marriage, to the tune of celebrating thirty-two years of marital union, if the Lord wills, come August 27, 2020.

This worldview borrows from the wisdom contained in the Serenity Prayer. I delight in this particular version:

> God, grant me the serenity to accept
> the things I cannot change,
> Courage to change the things I can,
> And wisdom to know the difference.

I most likely was heading toward divorce in the early years of my marriage. Strictly due to the fact I was only able to view my frustrations through the lens of what my wife, Monique, was doing or was not doing, from my perspective. I only saw the issues through the lens of my own myopism, which is the *modus operandi* of the average spouse. I often jest people would find me a most unpopular marriage counselor. I would be ruthless when one spouse would attempt to start to harp on their spouse's perceived inadequacies. I would immediately cut them off with a curt remark like, "We will deal with "so-and-so" later, but right now, I want to hone in on you for now. What do you understand as your contribution to the reasons we are meeting today?"

I share this part of your life, not because I am all that excited with sharing intimate details about my personal life. I do so because I know I am not alone in this erroneous understanding of our need for personal accountability. Regrettably, I lost so much valuable time early on in my marriage because of my erroneous worldview.

Again, as an Evangelical, I was intellectually aware of what the Bible taught about personal accountability, yet I did a *poor piss* job of connecting the dots and translating that cognitive awareness into the proper volitional practice. That is the essence of what I understand to be happening with my African American Evangelical brethren in their political engagement.

Many in the African American Evangelical community understand what the Bible teaches on a given matter, and they would heartily affirm it. They attend Church on a regular basis, with many attending Sunday school and various Bible studies throughout the week. I am sure many read their Bibles on a regular basis and would be able to pass a theological examination. So the issue is not one of a lack of intellectual acumen. The solution is not the need for more education. The solution is actually quite simple. It is first understanding *what* the Bible teaches and *then* correctly applying that understood truth to the applicable situation. It is the proper application to what the Bible teaches that I challenge my African American Evangelical brethren to come to understand and then, most importantly, to respond accordingly, to respond biblically.

If there is even one young single male who reads this and grows in his walk with God as a result, then the sharing of this intimate detail of my past marital struggles will be well worth the price of admission. By golly, if it were only to help my son, Ricky Jr., then it would still be well worth it. Yet I have relative intellectual certitude many, many males (my primary focus as helping other males should be the primary focus of all males), as well as females, could be helped immensely in navigating the travails of marriage. It should be noted this principle of personal accountability is readily applicable to countless other situations and especially in the area of relationships. It will not necessarily alleviate problems; my marriage *still* has *all* the typical relational trials and tribulations. This understanding has not necessarily changed my spouse. What has changed is how I respond and process the issues associated with interacting with her.

What could be the possible connection to this digression and American African Evangelical political engagement? I want to stress to my readers at the end of the day, the individual African American Evangelical is wholly responsible for how they chose to engage politically. The responsibility, while influenced by other factors, can *never* ultimately be attributed to factors like tradition, history, familial environment, pastoral guidance, etc., etc.

Why do I speak in such stark and definitive terms? Because the Holy Writ speaks in such stark and absolute terms. Need I remind the reader the Holy Writ expressly says, *"Study to shew **thyself** approved unto God, a workman that needeth not to be ashamed, rightly dividing the word of truth"* (2 Timothy 2:15, emphasis mine).

Yes, we desperately need the Church to equip us; we need the man of God to feed us the Bread of Heaven, Evangelicals are wholly dependent upon the Body of Christ to come alongside us that we may be presented mature in Christ at His coming (Colossians 1:28). All of these things and so more are true, but the fact still remains the individual Evangelical must *study* (as opposed to merely reading). The spotlight is placed squarely on the individual. The Holy Scriptures admonish every Evangelical that they must become convinced in their own mind (Romans 14:5).

Consequently, I want to speak directly to you if you are African American and consider yourself an Evangelical. If so, you are likely part of the 94 percent that voted for President Obama and the 88 percent who chose to vote for Hilary Rodman Clinton. How do you justify such a decision? I ask directly, yet I ask with a sense of fear and trembling. I personally invite you to join the dialogue and enter into the conversation. Even God sees this as a wise course of action as He expressly communicated to the Israelites through the prophet Isaiah, *"Come now, let us reason together, say the Lord; though your sins are like scarlet, they shall be white as snow; though they are red like crimson, they shall become like wool"* (Isaiah 1:18).

Yet I believe it important to note the prophet Isaiah goes on to reveal the Israelites must be willing and obedient. If they refused, then God promised the Israelites would be eaten by the sword, and this promise was no idle threat, for Isaiah reveals, *"For the mouth of the Lord has spoken"* (Isaiah 1:20). To the degree I am rightly dividing the Word of God, for some, eternity literally hangs in the balance and even for those whose eternity does not hang in the balance, they become subject to discipline in this life as well as the loss of reward in the next. If this does not arrest the attention of the reader then I can only say, "Lord, have mercy" to that individual. As one of my students is quick to say when he is flustered and seeks to capitulate intellectually, "I have nothing."

So now, please let me continue to press my case. Evangelicals exclusively possess the promise from God, if we take an honest accounting of our standing before Him and find ourselves outside His will, then divine relief, is graciously made available. God most graciously offers fallen humanity this divine rescue most vividly in the Epistle of the Apostle John when he writes, *"If we confess **our** sins, He is faithful and just to forgive us our sins and to cleanse us from all unrighteousness"* (1 John 1:9). Yet it is vitally important to caution the reader this is a conditional promise; it is wholly contingent upon the Evangelical taking decisive action.

Given the close proximity of the upcoming General Elections in November 2020, there is no time like the present to take stock of the issue and make serious inquiry of how our theology should shape how we engage politically from this point forward. That is precisely what I did after voting for William Jefferson Clinton in 1996. Up until that point, I had always voted Democratic. It was all I knew; everyone I knew of any consequence voted Democratic. My parents and my significant family members voted Democratic. When political candidates were blessed with opportunities to speak at our Churches, they were always from the Democratic Party. Granted, that was heavily influenced due to the fact I grew up in Chicago, but that was still my reality. So the Democratic Party became the ingrained consciousness of every African American to include yours truly. I remember even as I was in college, there was only a couple of African Americans I personally knew who choose to identify with the Republican Party. I believe they only did so as an opportunity to be different and gather attention. I know for a fact both of these individuals no longer have any affiliation with the Republican Party.

So I write as one who is intimately familiar with the African American political tradition, circa twentieth century. Yet the Evangelical has a clear biblical mandate. That mandate is one my momma was fond of repeatedly reminding my brothers and me, "once you know better, you have to do better." I realize it is highly unlikely (though with God all things are possible) all 94 percent of the African American Evangelical community will perform a 180 and not vote for the Democratic Party in the 2020 Presidential election but I would ask as a legitimate first step for all committed and sincere African American Evangelicals to simply earnestly pause, reflect and to pray.

Prayer for the Evangelical is the unique divine privilege of entering into an actual conversation with the very God of Heaven and Earth. Evangelicals have the unique privilege of entering the very throne room of heaven with our petitions. *Believers having direct access to heaven* is so mind-blogging it is truly inexplicable Evangelicals do not take more advantage of this precious commodity, and I heartily confess I am amongst the chief culprits. *The Bible informs the Evangelicals,* if things ever become hazy for us and we sense we are losing our way, or we don't know which direction to take all the Evangelical has to do is pour out their heart to God. James, the elder brother of Jesus Christ, writes in his Epistle under the inspiration of the Holy Spirit, *"If any of you lack wisdom, let him ask of God, that giveth to all men liberally and upbraideth not; and it shall be given him"* (James 1:5).

Frankly, we only have not because we ask not, and when we do ask amiss, meaning we are asking for the wrong things (James 4:3). There is so much despair and dysfunction in the African American community, but just as the story of the Prodigal Father reveals God the Father eagerly waits for us to "come to ourselves" and run back home. Believe me, my fellow African American brethren, the Father will not assume the posture of the pious elder brother. The Father will *anthropomorphically* raise up his garments and run eagerly to meet us at first sight of any of us turning to Him in repentance.[58]

There was a pastor who was counseling a couple who were experiencing trouble in their marital. The husband took the usual route of a disenchanted husband and vented his frustrations at all the things his wife was not doing that he felt she should have been doing and at all the things she was doing, the things he felt she should not have been doing (haven't we heard about this somewhere before). After listening intently to the husband getting off his chest, all the venom welling up in his spirit, the pastor calmly asked the husband a straightforward question. The pastor asked, "Are you praying for your wife?" The calm and loving demeanor of the pastor, coupled

---

[58] Anthropomorphism is the attribution of human traits, emotions, or intentions to non-human entities.

with the pride crushing nature of the question, pierced the soul of the husband to the marrow. You may have already guessed the husband was, yep, *yours truly*. The pastor went on to share it is nearly impossible to remain in conflict with someone you are earnestly praying for God's best for them.

Think about someone you may now be or were in the recent past in conflict with, no matter how huge or insignificant the issue. Now, imagine or even take the bold steps to pray and seek genuinely God's very best for that very person. I challenge anyone to commit to that spiritual discipline and not experience a spiritual transformation that replaces bitterness with compassion, replaces the pain with spiritual contentment replaces anger with peace.

I challenge the African American Evangelical specifically and all others in general to take this challenge. Concerning the others, in general, it would not have to be associated with your political engagement (though it most certainly could, and you would benefit) but consistent with the theme of this book, I want African American Evangelicals to narrow their focus and deal with the topic at hand: their political engagement, namely how they choose to vote in Presidential elections. Though I certainly grant even the African American Evangelical could most certainly apply this spiritual discipline to other aspects of their lives.

With all of these caveats acknowledged, let us now turn back to the task at hand. I am supremely confident if African American Evangelicals would pray something along these lines:

"Search me, O God, and know my heart; Try me, and know my anxieties; And see if there is any wicked way in me, And lead me in the way everlasting" (Psalm 139:23–24) that God will respond in ways beyond our imagination.

I am careful at this point to not to attempt to speculate how exactly God will respond but respond is one thing the Evangelical can be sure God will do. In fact, by God's providence, my Bible reading today (March 28, 2020) contained the following declaration from God, *"Before they call I will answer; while they are yet speaking, I will hear,"* (Isaiah 65:24). Now, while God made this promise to the Nation of Israel through the prophet Isaiah some seven hundred years before the birth of Jesus Christ, it still possesses applicability to New Testament believers. Israel was uniquely in a position for this gracious provision from God because they were His covenant people in the Old Testament. Evangelicals (remember, this is *my* preferred term to refer to believers in this current time period) are the New Testament equivalents to the Nation of Israel. Just as they were the covenant people in the Old Testament Evangelicals are the covenant people of God in the New Testament.

Just as it very difficult to imagine a husband truly maintaining a hostile posture toward his wife if he is indeed pouring out his heart in prayer *for* her, it is difficult imagining the heart of God not responding in favor toward the person pouring out their soul in earnest, prayerful supplication to gain God's insight as to how to proceed politically as an Evangelical. That is just what biblical wisdom is understood to be. It is thinking God's thought after Him; it is seeing things from His perspective. So although I will not in any way attempt to believe I can predict how or what God will respond in a given situation, the Bible reveals Jesus Christ in His current ministry role as our Great High Priest, "*ever liveth to make intercession for them* [Evangelicals]" (Hebrews 7:25).

Next, African American Evangelicals need to demand more, more from themselves and definitely more from their leaders. Concerning leaders, that may necessitate more formal education and while a formal education is not certainly never to be the sole consideration, there remains a high premium on an educated clergy. The African American Church has by in large allowed the pendulum to swing too much in the direction of elevating the position of Pastor or in the term more African Americans are familiar with, *Reverend.*

The Bible clearly presents a legitimate expression of respect for the man of God in the local place of worship, but the Bible equally posits the tension of the pastor assuming the role of Servant Leader. Boy, if there were ever two words that seem to be joined together but possessing a logical contradiction, it would be the phrase *Servant Leader*, yet the Word of God does just that.

You attend the typical African American Church, and just driving in the Church parking lot, one quickly recognizes the over-inflated status of hierarchy in the typical African American Church. The Pastor has his assigned parking spot strategically located close to the front entrance (and the new trend is for the *First Lady*, i.e., pastor's wife, to have her own parking spot). I fondly remember someone sharing the story of a Pastor of a megachurch, which was so large they had to provide shuttle service to drive parishioners from their vehicle in the parking lot to the place of worship. Yet where did the Pastor of this megachurch park his vehicle? He usually parked it at a location far from the Church and rode the shuttle just like all the other members of the Church. That act alone beautifully illustrates the concept of Servant Leadership. When I grew up, when we would have Church dinners, no one would eat until the Pastor was seated and served first. I found this odd, especially when I became an adult and joined the military, where the Army taught us and trained us that officers always ate last even though they possessed the highest rank and retained the most authority.

You attend the average African American Church, and upon entering the sanctuary, you immediately know where the position of authority resides. *Evangelicals hold that it is the* pulpit. It is such a venerated place that no layperson is allowed to enter unless you are the Pastor's nurse, and she only enters to cater to his needs with water, handkerchiefs, mints, or his robe. If you have an announcement, there is usually a microphone set up off to the side where you could address the body. One particular Pastor instituted a practice where the entire congregation would rise upon his entrance into the sanctuary, much like when a judge enters the courtroom. I especially found this a strange practice because the Pastor would always enter the service about ten to twelve minutes *after* the service began. I never understood why he was not part of the entire worship service, just like the rest of us.

So respect for the Man of God, no problem! The Bible clearly commands and expects Evangelicals to do so cheerfully and as an act of worship. Yet I point out the fact that the Bible makes that not many in the Evangelical community seem to understand. The Apostle Paul makes a special point to reveal under the inspiration of the Holy Spirit that Evangelicals are to place a special emphasis of attention, not on the prominent parts of the body, but Evangelicals are to lavish attention on the part of the less honorable body part (1 Corinthians 12:21ff.).

As a result, as one example of displaying fidelity to this principle, whenever I host a function at my residence, I make a practice of ensuring those who seem to be living on the margins are the first person I invite and pay special attention to during the event. If and when applicable, I ask the Pastor, but I treat him and place him on the same level as any other member of the body. I remember when I was younger and served as the head of our Church's search committee. After we selected the new pastor, I was teaching Sunday school the following Sunday. I knew the tendency of African American Evangelical's overemphasis on the role of the pastor, so I made the following bold declaration and timed it just as our new pastor arrived that Sunday morning. I said, "If I were to ask who the most important member of the Church is to stand, either ALL of us had to stand, or NOBODY stands."

I admit I purposely made a big theatric presentation of the matter, but I made my point, a point I wanted to make to everyone present during that Sunday school class to include our new Pastor understood. The average African American Evangelical Church is riddled with a climate of "big I's" and "little u's" and the person in the pew does not seem to realize this is, in the main, a self-inflicted wound, especially in Baptist and other Evangelical denomination that possess a Congregation-led polity.[59]

In spite of the Bible's clear and unmistakable message of servanthood, the quest for power is rampant. If it is not the Pastor, it seems to be the Deacon Board, or if not the Deacon Board, it is some influential section, usually tied to money or family lineage. My point is regardless of the source it is still true that a pursuit for *who is in charge* is utterly foolish as the only person who is genuinely in charge is the *head*, and like my momma used to say, *"anything with two heads*

---

[59] There are four general types of polity in churches today. Church polity refers to how a church's leadership is structured. The congregational model has the authority resting in the congregation. For more details, see www.gotquestions.org/church-polity.html.

is a monster. "The Body of Christ has only one head, and He is Jesus Christ of Nazareth (Colossians 1:18).

I believe the whole insidious culture of *whooping* is the result of a vicious circle. Preachers fall prey to it because it is what they understand that is what the people want and if they are going to be relevant and employable; then they have to give the people what they crave. The person in the pew sees the 'happening" congregations with these slick, smooth-talking charismatic communicators and they sense they need to acquire one if their Church is to become the *new happening place.*

Congregants leave these places of worship emotionally sated but intellectually and volitionally void. They have zeal in spade, but they are still people with zeal but without knowledge (Romans 10:2). The Adversary has no issue whatsoever with people who leave the house of worship but possess no spiritual armor. As a result, we have soldiers arriving at the front line but possessing no military accouterment. They have no breastplate, no helmet, no sword; they do not even possess five smooth stones.

Much like Goliath, the *Forces of Darkness* have no fear whatsoever as they understand their opponents are truly impotent. The *Forces of Darkness* use the same type of guile the Serpent employed in the garden with Eve. Even though God admonishes Evangelicals not to become beguiled and led astray, we are because we imbibe the message from the secular culture rather than the Word of God.

The Word of God posits the sanctity of life all the way from the cradle to natural death. Still, many Evangelicals brazenly embrace the Democratic Party's worldview that it is a *woman's choice* even as the Holy Scriptures teach redeemed Evangelical Females that God has bought them from Satan's slave marketplace of sin. The Bible explicitly teaches their bodies have bought them and are no longer their own (1 Corinthians 6:20). The Word of God posits marriage to be the union of one man and one woman for life, but many Evangelicals accept a political party's worldview that marriage is malleable to the whims of the culture (Genesis 2:14, Matthew 19:5). The Word of God posits that gender is the beautiful gift to mankind from its Creator to promote human flourishing and to fulfill the mandate to fill the Earth while many Evangelicals accepts a political party's worldview that gender is a social construct and not to be understood in binary terms.

These false worldviews are able to flourish because the only vaccine made available to Evangelicals is the Word of God. The Word of God preached Expositionally, the Word of God preached Christologically, the Word of God, preached Hermeneutically, the Word of God preached Evangelistically. None of these pursuits will likely be secured when the focus of the preaching centers around *whooping*. Evangelicals do not need more emotive stimulation; they need more intellectual stimulation. Please note, I am not advocating for *no emotive stimulus*. I would be the first to depart a Church that possessed no emotive fervor in their worship. Evangelicals are explicitly admonished by Jesus Christ that He is seeking only those who worship Him in *Spirit* and Truth.

The truth seems to be a fleeting proposition, both in the culture (which should cause no surprise or produce no consternation) but more tragically inside the one place, it should be safeguarded to the death: The Evangelical Church, which should be of grave concern and much fear. There are some things that are worth falling upon our swords. Evangelicals, throughout the history of the Church, have always passionately believed they are some hills that worth dying for and over. Life, marriage, and gender are the three things that are not part of the fuzzy math; they are not hazy; they are not nebulous; they are not inconsequential. They are often both literal and eternal in their implications.

Although I seek to close on a positive, I must again remind the reader, the decisions we make today derive from some worldview. For one to attempt to posit he has no worldview is only to demonstrate his worldview, feeble and inept as such a worldview would be. Orthopraxy always follows proper orthodoxy and a proper orthodoxy always necessarily follows a solid, biblically-based worldview. Jesus Christ stated this truth this way:

> Even so every good tree bringeth forth good
> fruit; but a corrupt tree bringeth forth evil fruit.

> A good tree cannot bring forth evil, neither can
> a corrupt tree bring forth good fruit. Every tree
> that bringeth not forth good fruit is hewn down,
> and cast into the fire. Wherefore by their fruits ye
> shall know them. (Matthew 17–20)

All of this is to say God commands every Evangelical to make their election and calling sure (2 Peter 1:10). In fact, the Apostle Peter implored his readers to give diligence toward the matter. The reason why should be painfully apparent to anyone with even a smattering of brainpower. The final destination of Heaven or Hell are the stakes. Proper alignment with political engagement does not earn anyone salvation, but proper alignment with political engagement most certainly does flow from salvation.

Yet I equally say many in the professing African American Church are, in fact, not genuinely saved. I make this bold declaration without any specific person in mind and with no secret agenda. I only state what God authorizes every Evangelical to state because of God's own self-revelation. The Apostle Paul wrote, *"But in a great house there are not only vessels of gold and of silver, but also of wood and of earth; and some to honour, and some to dishonour"* (2 Timothy 2:20). Christ is even more emphatic when He said in His parable of the Wheat and the Tares:

> Let both [wheat and tares] grow until the
> harvest: and in the time of harvest I will say to
> the reapers, Gather ye together first the tares, and
> bind them in bundles to burn them; but gather
> the wheat in my barn. (Matthew 13:30)

I write as one with a heavy heart. I wish there were no need for a book dealing with a topic such as this. I wish African American Evangelicals would come to realize all of our Evangelical life is to be lived out under the rubric of biblical revelation. There is no compartmentalization of the Evangelical life. Jesus Christ is *Lord* over all dimensions of the Evangelical experience.

I say to my fellow African American Evangelicals we have not simply because we have asked not. We *ask* of Jesus Christ all the while we *demand* from our preachers they feed us lean meat and not the drippings from the fat of the meat. We demand they feed us Christ and His Gospel, but we can only demand when we know what the demand will look like when God speaks from His perch from the heavenlies. We must make this demand upon ourselves and our clergy a *sine qua non* and we must do so realizing it will be long, and it will be painful, and it will be hard.

I close by remembering the words of President John F. Kennedy as the US committed to reaching the Moon before the Soviets. He galvanized the country with these poignant words, "We choose to go to the Moon in this decade and do the other things, not because they are easy, but because they are hard, because that goal will serve to organize and measure the best of our energies and skills, because that challenge is one that we are willing to accept, one we are unwilling to postpone, and one which we intend to win, and others, too."

I write as one professing African American Evangelical speaking earnestly and with all the best of intentions to my fellow professing African American Evangelicals. I write with the full awareness of what I yearn to see take place in the greater African American Evangelical community will be daunting and beyond human strength and ingenuity. But the Evangelical need not despair as these are just the type of pursuits we know if we are to succeed, it will only be due to the miraculous enablement of power from on high.

I know I have not been 100 percent precise in all of my conclusions and attempts at theological insights. Insofar as I have been consistent with the revelation of Holy Scriptures, then to God be the glory and the gates of Hell be damned. For those areas where I have not cut the mustard then as the saints used to say as I was growing up, "Charge it to my head, not to my heart." My only hope in writing this book is that God is glorified and God's people are conformed to the image of His dear Son.

Well, it is later in the evening than when we first began. One day the Sun will set never to arise ever again. I look forward to going home on that final evening train. Only eternity will reveal as to the degree of success I will have achieved in the noble pursuit of finishing out my fourth quarter strong. Until then, to my fellow Evangelicals, *Keep Your Hands to the Plow and Seek to Serve for an Audience of One.* My earnest pray as well as solemn warning is every professing Evangelical reading this would not be found *Weighed and Wanting.*

ABOUT THE AUTHOR

Dr. Ricky Verndale Kyles Sr. is a proud graduate of The Southern Baptist Theological Seminary, earning a Doctor of Educational Ministry degree. He currently resides in the great state of Texas after completing a twenty-eight career in the US Army where he retired with the rank of Lieutenant Colonel.

Dr. Kyles was born in Brooksville, Mississippi, and grew up on the Southside of Chicago, Illinois. He has spent the majority of his formative time being a member of and worshipping in predominantly African American Churches ranging in positions from Sunday school teacher to Christian Education Direction as well as serving as Pastor-Teacher.

Thus, this book is not some outsider critiquing some entity which the critiquer has no familiarity. No, this is written from an insider's perspective who longs, as the Apostle Paul longed for his countrymen, that African Americans be saved and walk in the newness of life. Dr. Kyles submits there can be no *newness of life* when African American Evangelicals align themselves with political candidates that support abortion on demand, redefine marriage, and reject the traditional understanding of gender.

Dr. Kyles is not timid when he postulates it is not theologically permissible for *any* committed Evangelical to vote for *any* candidate from the Democratic Party as presently constituted. He feels compelled to write to raise a clarion call to *all* serious-minded African American Evangelicals it is high time we match our correct doctrine (orthodoxy) with correct practices (orthopraxy).

CPSIA information can be obtained
at www.ICGtesting.com
Printed in the USA
LVHW110540100721
692281LV00005B/581

9 781644 687895